The Necessity of Aesthetic Education

Bloomsbury Philosophy of Education

Series Editor: Michael Hand

Bloomsbury Philosophy of Education is an international research series dedicated to the examination of conceptual and normative questions raised by the practice of education. There is a particular focus on philosophical dimensions of current policy debates, though work of a less applied nature will also have a place.

Editorial Board:
Sigal Ben-Porath (University of Pennsylvania, USA)
Randall Curren (University of Rochester, USA)
Doret de Ruyter (Vrije Universiteit Amsterdam, the Netherlands)
Dianne Gereluk (University of Calgary, Canada)
Judith Suissa (UCL Institute of Education, UK)
Christopher Winch (King's College London, UK)

Also available in the series:
Why Teach Philosophy in Schools?, Jane Gatley
Wonder and Education, Anders Schinkel
Cherishing and the Good Life of Learning, Ruth Cigman
A Critique of Pure Teaching Methods and the Case of Synthetic Phonics, Andrew Davis
Philosophical Reflections on Neuroscience and Education, William H. K
Children, Religion and the Ethics of Influence, John Tillson

The Necessity of Aesthetic Education

The Place of the Arts on the Curriculum

Laura D'Olimpio

BLOOMSBURY ACADEMIC
LONDON • NEW YORK • OXFORD • NEW DELHI • SYDNEY

BLOOMSBURY ACADEMIC
Bloomsbury Publishing Plc, 50 Bedford Square, London, WC1B 3DP, UK
Bloomsbury Publishing Inc, 1359 Broadway, New York, NY 10018, USA
Bloomsbury Publishing Ireland, 29 Earlsfort Terrace, Dublin 2, D02 AY28, Ireland

BLOOMSBURY, BLOOMSBURY ACADEMIC and the Diana logo
are trademarks of Bloomsbury Publishing Plc

First published in Great Britain 2024
This paperback edition published in 2026

Copyright © Laura D'Olimpio, 2024

Laura D'Olimpio has asserted her right under the Copyright, Designs and Patents Act, 1988, to be
identified as Author of this work.

For legal purposes the Acknowledgements on pp. x–xi constitute an
extension of this copyright page.

Series design: Clare Turner

All rights reserved. No part of this publication may be: i) reproduced or transmitted in any form, electronic or mechanical, including photocopying, recording or by means of any information storage or retrieval system without prior permission in writing from the publishers; or ii) used or reproduced in any way for the training, development or operation of artificial intelligence (AI) technologies, including generative AI technologies. The rights holders expressly reserve this publication from the text and data mining exception as per Article 4(3) of the Digital Single Market Directive (EU) 2019/790.

Bloomsbury Publishing Plc does not have any control over, or responsibility for, any third-party websites referred to or in this book. All internet addresses given in this book were correct at the time of going to press. The author and publisher regret any inconvenience caused if addresses have changed or sites have ceased to exist, but can accept no responsibility for any such changes.

A catalogue record for this book is available from the British Library.

Library of Congress Cataloging-in-Publication Data
Names: D'Olimpio, Laura, author.
Title: The necessity of aesthetic education : the place of the arts on the curriculum / Laura D'Olimpio.
Description: London ; New York : Bloomsbury Academic, 2024. | Series: Bloomsbury philosophy of education | Includes bibliographical references and index. | Summary: "Laura D'Olimpio argues that aesthetic education ought to be a compulsory part of education for all students, from pre-primary through to high school, as it is essential that young people have the opportunity to make art, experience and understand art and be informed as to the artistic history and aesthetic theories that have shaped their own culture and others. The book defends arts education on the basis of art's distinctive value and centrality to human experience. It also engages with topics such as the art teacher's role in the classroom, curricula concerns and gleaning moral meanings from artworks"– Provided by publisher.
Identifiers: LCCN 2023052856 (print) | LCCN 2023052857 (ebook) |
ISBN 9781350120907 (hardback) | ISBN 9781350224971 (paperback) |
ISBN 9781350120921 (epub) | ISBN 9781350120914 (ebook)
Subjects: LCSH: Aesthetics–Study and teaching. | Arts–Study and teaching.
Classification: LCC BH61 .D65 2024 (print) | LCC BH61 (ebook) |
DDC 701/.17071–dc23/eng/20231205
LC record available at https://lccn.loc.gov/2023052856
LC ebook record available at https://lccn.loc.gov/2023052857

ISBN:	HB:	978-1-3501-2090-7
	PB:	978-1-3502-2497-1
	ePDF:	978-1-3501-2091-4
	eBook:	978-1-3501-2092-1

Series: Bloomsbury Philosophy of Education

Typeset by Integra Software Services Pvt. Ltd.

For product safety related questions contact productsafety@bloomsbury.com.

To find out more about our authors and books visit www.bloomsbury.com
and sign up for our newsletters.

For artists and art-lovers

Contents

Series editor's foreword		viii
Acknowledgements		x
Introduction		1
1	Arts education in policy and practice	9
2	Why value the arts and arts education?	35
3	Defending arts education	53
4	The centrality of aesthetic experience	75
5	Objections and replies	95
6	Instrumental defences of arts education	111
7	Aesthetics and ethics	131
Conclusion: The necessity of aesthetic education		147
Notes		151
References		154
Index		166

Series editor's foreword

Bloomsbury Philosophy of Education is an international research series dedicated to the examination of conceptual and normative questions raised by the practice of education.

Philosophy of education is a branch of philosophy rooted in and attentive to the practical business of educating people. Those working in the field are often based in departments of education rather than departments of philosophy; many have experience of teaching in primary or secondary schools; and all seek to contribute in some way to the improvement of educational interactions, institutions or ideals. Like philosophers of other stripes, philosophers of education are prone to speculative flight, and the altitudes they reach are occasionally dizzying; but their inquiries begin and end on the ground of educational practice, with matters of immediate concern to teachers, parents, administrators and policymakers.

Two kinds of question are central to the discipline. *Conceptual* questions have to do with the language we use to formulate educational aims and describe educational processes. At least some of the problems we encounter in our efforts to educate arise from conceptual confusion or corruption – from what Wittgenstein called 'the bewitchment of our intelligence by means of language'. Disciplined attention is needed to such specifically educational concepts as learning and teaching, schooling and socializing, training and indoctrinating, but also to the wider conceptual terrain in which educational discourse sits: what is it to be a person, or to have a mind, or to know or think or flourish, or to be rational, intelligent, autonomous or virtuous? *Normative* questions have to do with the justification of educational norms, aims and policies. What educators do is guided and constrained by principles, goals, imperatives and protocols that may or may not be ethically defensible or appropriate to the task in hand. Philosophers of education interrogate the normative infrastructure of educational practice, with a view to exposing its deficiencies and infirmities and drawing up blueprints for its repair or reconstruction. Frequently, of course, the two kinds of question overlap: inappropriate aims sometimes rest on conceptual muddles, and our understanding of educational concepts is liable to distortion by ill-founded pedagogical norms.

In terms of scholarly output, philosophy of education is in rude health. The field supports half a dozen major international journals, numerous learned societies and a busy annual calendar of national and international conferences. At present, however, too little of this scholarly output finds a wider audience, and too few of the important ideas introduced in journal articles are expanded into fully developed theories. The aim of this book series is to identify the best new work in the field and encourage its authors to develop, defend and work out the implications of their ideas, in a way that is accessible to a broad readership.

It is hoped that volumes in the series will be of interest not only to scholars and students of philosophy of education and neighbouring branches of philosophy, but also to the wider community of educational researchers, practitioners and policymakers. All volumes are written for an international audience: while some authors begin with the way an educational problem has been framed in a particular national context, it is the problem itself, not the local framing of it, on which the ensuing arguments bear.

Michael Hand

Acknowledgements

I have many people to thank for their engagement with the ideas I have shared in this book. In earlier formats, I have been supported – usually through challenging questioning (a true sign of philosophical respect!) – by those who have read drafts of my chapters or heard presentations and talks I have given on this topic. These talks and the questions and feedback I received have all helped push my thinking, forcing me to further clarify and justify my claims, ultimately strengthening my arguments.

I started working on this book when I undertook my first sabbatical in mid-2018 at Teacher's College, Columbia University in New York City, USA. I remember conducting my literature review as the summer heat kept me in the air-conditioned library and the Starbucks on campus as I discovered the joy of iced oat milk chai lattes – a habit that did not make it beyond American borders … It seems fitting that I completed the manuscript while on my second sabbatical in early 2023 at the University of Canterbury in Christchurch, New Zealand. My thanks to the Philosophy of Education programme at TC, to Megan Laverty and David Hansen in particular, and to UC and the School of Educational Studies and Leadership for awarding me a Visiting Canterbury Fellowship. The support and collegiality that accompanied these two research fellowships, along with the time off from my teaching and administrative duties, cannot be underestimated in helping me to ultimately complete this work.

I am grateful to the Jubilee Centre for Character and Virtues at the University of Birmingham, who invited me to talk upon the commencement of my position at the University of Birmingham in 2019. I am also grateful to the Philosophy of Education Society of Great Britain (PESGB) who invited me to give the keynote at their annual conference in 2020. That, of course, ended up being delivered online in 2021, after the pandemic delayed the event and national lockdowns forced us all online and indoors. The pandemic also slowed my productivity and, as a result, this book took longer to complete than I had originally anticipated. But just as we got through the pandemic in the end, despite losing some significant and beautiful souls along the way (including my Nanna, my father and my uncle), and I finally managed to return to my homeland of Australia after the borders had been closed for far too long, so too have I managed to finish this monograph!

A special thanks to Michael Hand, Andrew Peterson, Christoph Teschers and Jeff Standley for commenting on draft versions of my chapters, and for discussing ideas with me and encouraging me in this project. Thanks also to Grace Lockrobin, who has always enthusiastically encouraged my work on aesthetics and that has helped me feel as though an audience was waiting to read this work. I found that encouraging, if not slightly daunting, but it helped most when the pandemic made me feel quite isolated and shut off from the world. Another thank you to Michael for helping me survive the pandemic as my partner in work and life.

Some aspects of Chapters 2, 4 and 7 have appeared in print in journal articles. I would like to acknowledge and give my thanks to Sage, Wiley and Taylor and Francis for permission to reproduce these here, in slightly altered, expanded forms. A version of Chapter 2 appeared in the *British Journal of Educational Studies*:

> D'Olimpio, L (2021). Defending Aesthetic Education. *British Journal of Educational Studies*. DOI:10.1080/00071005.2021.1960267 copyright © Society for Educational Studies, reprinted by permission of Taylor & Francis Ltd., http://www.tandfonline.com on behalf of Society for Educational Studies.

A version of Chapter 4 appeared in the *Journal of Philosophy of Education*, which resulted from the keynote I gave to the PESGB:

> D'Olimpio, L. (2022). Aesthetica and *eudaimonia*: Education for Flourishing Must Include the Arts. *Journal of Philosophy of Education*. DOI:10.1111/1467-9752.12661

And Chapter 7 draws upon an article published in *Theory and Research in Education*:

> D'Olimpio, L. (2020). When Good Art Is Bad: Educating the Critical Viewer, *Theory and Research in Education*, 18(2): pp. 137–50. Copyright © 2020 (SAGE Journals). DOI: https://doi.org/10.1177/1477878520947024

Lastly, I must thank my mum, Grace, who raised me surrounded by art and cultivated within me a love for creative expression in many different media. My mum was an artist – a ceramicist – who was also involved in supporting the multicultural arts from when I was young. I was a part of this awe-inspiring world of art and beauty growing up, which has influenced my belief that the arts are truly such an important part of life and that all children should have the same opportunities to play with art and learn to appreciate artworks. I love that Mum is still an enthusiastic reader of my work and I know she will find this book particularly meaningful.

Introduction

The Necessity of Aesthetic Education is a manifesto. Here I will make and defend a philosophical argument for the necessity of arts education for all school-aged students, from pre-primary to high school, on the basis of its distinctive value. Such an argument is timely, given the so-called crisis in the arts and humanities, with declining student numbers in subjects that do not have a direct vocational correlative, and increased focus on science, technology, engineering and mathematics (STEM) subjects, further borne out by funding cuts to the arts and the humanities and a public and political rhetoric that does not seem to value them. There is a need to argue for why the arts and arts education are valuable, for their own sake, as well as for the positive contributions they can and do make to society. While focussing on defending the intrinsic value of the arts and arts education, I also note the positive benefits they have instrumentally, contributing to other goods in society and to the lives of individuals.

I claim that art and, by extension, arts education, including the aesthetic expression and experience of creating and engaging with art is intrinsically valuable. That which is expressed through art, through the many various and diverse art forms and media, is uniquely and essentially valuable to the lived human experience and thus, everyone should have the opportunity to access and understand such aesthetic experience. In its creation and reception, as a form of self-expression, imaginative engagement, cognitive as well as affective experience, source of individual and social reflection and contemplation, art has always been central to human life. The arts capture and express something that is irreducible to other forms of knowledge and, as such, is deemed aesthetically valuable.

The *aesthetic* is a philosophical concept that is grounded in a historical, social context. Aesthetic values have been shaped and informed by theory and practice, and they change with time. This can be seen in the movement away from 'beauty' as a necessary formal feature in art, along with various beauty standards that alter according to changing tastes and social mores. In order to fully appreciate and gain the most out of the arts, which offer a variety of aesthetic experience, there are concepts, skills and techniques integral to such understanding. As such, aesthetic education – which is arts education that includes the teaching of art theories and an accompanying understanding of relevant historical context – ought to be a compulsory part of education for all students. It is essential that young people, from pre-primary through to high school, have the opportunity to make art, experience and understand art and be informed as to the artistic history and aesthetic theories that have shaped their own culture as well as that of others.

This book is divided into seven chapters. Chapter 1 commences with an examination of arts education policy and practice. It includes a critical detailing of some examples of current arts educational policies and curricula in the developed Western world, considers their strengths and weaknesses, and asks whether arts education in practice aligns with what is promised in those policies. The arts are included on the national curricula for most developed Western countries, usually defended on the basis of their social, cultural and individual benefits. The value of the arts, particularly the visual arts, design and technology, drama, dance and music, is recognized in that they (or some combination thereof) are listed as mandatory subjects. Yet despite an often academically rigorous arts education curricula, the reality of which schools and students have access to good quality arts education is much less consistent with inequitable distributions of time, effort, space and resources across schools.

This is the chosen starting point for this book because arts education must be supported by good educational and governmental policy, quality resourcing and teacher training in order to be practically effective. With reference to arts education policies and practices in Australia, the United Kingdom and the United States of America, Chapter 1 critically examines how arts education is justified in primary and secondary schools and what these policies look like in practice. While education in the arts is often compulsory in these and other developed countries, there are gaps between policy and practice, between the glowing reports of the benefits of arts education for school-aged children and the reality of what they experience.

Most noticeably, there is an inequitable distribution of access to good quality arts education for all students with those in lower socio-economic demographics and ethnic minorities most obviously lacking the same opportunities as elsewhere. It is a shame that for those students who arguably most need the arts and who are the ones who are least likely to stumble upon incredible and meaningful experiences of engaging with and creating the arts in their own households and communities, their arts offerings at school are also likely to be diminutive. The defence I will mount in favour of aesthetic education for all school-aged students bears heavily upon the importance of redressing this imbalance.

Chapter 2 starts by defining two key concepts that I rely upon throughout this book; namely, 'art' and 'aesthetic experience'. It then considers a couple of prominent existing defences of teaching the arts in schools, drawing upon the justifications offered in arts educational policy and curricula. Educational curricula usually highlight the importance of the arts in terms of educating students in constructive and creative means for self-expression and advocating for the historical and cultural importance of the arts, which also ties to notions of identity and self-expression. While creative self-expression is on balance a valuable goal, and the arts do have historical and cultural significance, these are not the best defences of compulsory arts education. They may very well supplement the best defence of compulsory aesthetic education, but they fall short of supplying a convincing sufficient reason to teach the arts.

Another popular and rather convincing argument often made in defence of the arts connects artistic pursuits to the cultivation of certain virtuous habits. A common link can be seen to be made between literature and sympathy, with readers of novels praised for the practice and cultivation of what may be termed ethical attention. Thus, the two well-regarded arguments that seek to defend arts education that are focussed on for critique in this chapter include one that prioritizes the role art has to play in supporting self-expression. The second defence of the arts is made in relation to their role in supporting moral improvement. While I agree that the arts may very well provide useful modes for self-expression, and while I also see how narrative artworks in particular play a prominent and significant role in morally educating individuals and society, I will point out the weaknesses of these defences. Ultimately, I conclude, these defences will not do in our search for a robust justification for the necessity of compulsory aesthetic education. I am, however, happy for these arguments to be supplementary to my main defence that I outline in Chapter 4.

By this point, having ruled out a couple of extant defences of arts education as not viable for my purposes, I move on to consider the theories developed by Elliot Eisner and Maxine Greene – two significant American theorists who have helped shape and influence arts education policy and practice in important and positive ways over the past fifty years. Chapter 3 is devoted to detailing and critiquing the work and theories of Eisner and Greene because of the important roles they have had to play in shaping what we now think of as aesthetic education. Eisner in particular is a key figure associated with discipline-based art education (DBAE) and arts-based research, both of which now dominate approaches to arts education across the West. It is by building upon the work of people like Eisner and Greene that we continue to robustly and reasonably defend the role art can and does and should play in education, in our lives and in our society.

However, what will become apparent is that I do not follow Eisner or Greene's theories verbatim. Chapter 3 sees Eisner's and Greene's defences of aesthetic education charitably critiqued, and it is concluded that both offer what I call 'composite arguments' when defending what the arts and aesthetic education can and should do. I do not opt for a composite argument in defence of compulsory aesthetic education because I want a simple (*a la* Occam's razor), essentialist defence based on what is distinctive about the arts. While I see no problem with supplementary arguments being made in defence of the arts, I want one clear line of argument that defends aesthetic education based on what is uniquely valuable about the arts. It is this kind of justification that will be sound enough to support a case for compulsory education in the arts.

Chapter 4 details the book's central argument defending compulsory aesthetic education for all school-aged students. Education ought to support students to live meaningful, autonomous lives, filled with rich experiences. The arts and aesthetic education are vital to such flourishing lives in that they afford bold, beautiful, moving experiences of awe, wonder and the sublime that are connected to the central human functional capability Martha Nussbaum labels *Senses, Imagination, and Thought*. Drawing upon Denis Dutton, John Dewey and others, I claim that everyone has a natural instinct for art and a human capability connected to enjoying aesthetic experiences. Thus, everyone ought to have the opportunity to learn about art, to appreciate and to create art, to critique art and to understand how we are connected to the culture of our society. Here I detail my defence of compulsory aesthetic education across the curriculum on the basis of the aesthetic experiences the arts afford, and the central role such experiences play in the flourishing life.

Chapter 5 considers and responds to two possible objections that challenge the defence I offer of the necessity of aesthetic education based on the centrality of aesthetic experience to the meaningful life. The first objection, which I call the 'naturalistic' objection, is connected to the argument I have made about human persons having a natural instinct for art. If people naturally derive pleasure from the arts and nature instinctively, why do we need to educate them to receive aesthetic experiences? And, further, why do we need to educate them in the arts (as distinct from other sources of aesthetic experience)?

The second objection I consider I call the 'subjectivity' objection. The subjectivity challenge notes that one person's flourishing life may look quite different to another's and we must respect individual preferences and choices involved in the kinds of lives people choose to live. If we take personal autonomy seriously, this seems to imply respecting someone's choice when they claim they do not enjoy any arts activities and claim they may flourish without engaging with the arts. Can a fulfilled life include hobbies and forms of entertainment but exclude the arts? In this chapter, I will offer responses to both of these important objections.

As I have noted, I defend aesthetic education on the basis of an intrinsic defence of the arts, based on what is distinctively valuable about the arts. Yet it is also important to consider whether instrumental or extrinsic defences of the arts and arts education are harmful or dangerous to our focal cause or whether they may provide useful supplementary reasons why we should teach the arts in schools. With this in mind, in Chapter 6 I consider instrumental defences of aesthetic education. It is important to acknowledge the suspicion over instrumental arguments when it comes to defending the arts, education and arts education. There is a long-held wariness of and hostility to defending the arts in terms of extrinsic benefits or in instrumental terms. In this chapter I will consider this wariness and will endorse vigilance against reductively instrumentalist arguments whereby arts education serves narrowly extrinsic aims. However, I will ultimately conclude that not *all* instrumental arguments are to be rejected, and in fact, some may supplement and support the primary justification of aesthetic education which rests upon art's intrinsic value.

Given we have by now considered or briefly mentioned various values of the arts and of aesthetic education – be they aesthetic, economic, ethical, individual, social or political – it is worth thinking about how the art teacher might have to juggle these sometimes competing facets in the classroom. Chapter 7 critically engages with the tensions that arise between aesthetic and ethical values of artworks, particularly in relation to arts education. It will critique the position known as aestheticism, whereby aesthetes contend that any moral value of an artwork should not affect the work's overall value, which should be solely based upon its aesthetic value. It will compare aestheticism to the position defended by the ethicist, who adopts an all-things-considered perspective, claiming that the moral value of artworks can be gleaned, judged, and may affect the overall value of an artwork. This debate will be viewed through an educational lens, lending support to ethicism by considering educational implications of aestheticism and ethicism. It concludes that arts education should rightly teach students the skills of learning to appreciate art, and engaging both critically and in a receptive or sympathetic manner with artworks.

It is in the creative nature of artists and artworks to push social boundaries and offer new and sometimes challenging perspectives. Therefore, it is vitally important that students are taught to value the aesthetic and formal features of artworks and appreciate aesthetic experiences, while also learning they may, at the same time, be critical viewers and creators. An open, receptive and creative approach to art is at the heart of aesthetic education, but this should coexist with individual and collective criticality, even when such attitudes may yield competing messages. Arts teachers must be well trained precisely because aesthetic education involves many elements: arts creation and reception, and an understanding of relevant theory and historical context in relation to the artworks under consideration. Furthermore, each of the following elements – the skill of the artist, the presentation or display of the artwork, as well as the reception of the work, which includes the viewer's attitude – requires a form of learning, training or education.

While we want students to learn to be sympathetic interpreters of artworks, open to experiencing the aesthetic experiences on offer, we also need them to be critically engaged, which includes critically engaging with the ethical and political messages gleaned from art. This is the case to ensure they understand and appreciate the work, which includes understanding the context in which the work was created. While the teacher may bypass any moral risk by carefully selecting which artworks the students engage with, this does not then protect students when they are out on their own, encountering, engaging with and stumbling upon other artworks, including mass artworks and media.

Given that engaging with artworks is more or less unavoidable, we need to be well educated to receive them both critically and sympathetically. Art and design surround us, in public and private spaces, in the streets and through the technological devices to which we have constant access. Whether or not we acknowledge it, the messages, meanings and feelings conveyed through art, through the many various and diverse art forms and media, are uniquely and essentially valuable to the lived human experience. We cannot avoid the cultural zeitgeist, the significant personal encounters with artworks that have moved and motivated us, our shared aesthetic reference points, and strong reactions we have had to artworks to which we have been exposed: either willingly or circumstantially. Humans have a natural instinct for art and art has always been central to human life, playing many roles but essentially as sources of *aesthetic experience*. As such, this book defends the necessity of aesthetic education for all school-aged students, on the basis of the distinctive *aesthetic value* that art holds: the capacity to offer and create an aesthetic experience for those who engage with it.

1

Arts education in policy and practice

Introduction

The arts are at once celebrated and struggling – in society and in schools. Arts education policies in many countries, including Australia, Canada, Ireland, Aotearoa New Zealand, the UK and the United States of America, are starting to make the right kinds of claims in support of teaching the arts to primary and secondary school-aged students. They contain language expressing the value of the arts – socially, culturally, personally as well as educationally – and identify the visual arts, design and technology, drama, dance and music (or some combination thereof) as mandatory subjects. Yet the fate of the arts is often tied to political agendas which usually determine their presence, prominence and impact on the relevant educational budget spreadsheets and school timetables.

With reference to arts education policies and practices in Australia, the UK and the United States of America, this chapter will critically examine how arts education is justified in primary and secondary schools and what these policies look like in practice. Although these three countries will be my focus, some wider conclusions may be drawn as a result (Sharp & Métais, 2000: i). After conducting large-scale empirical research in the field across sixty countries for UNESCO, Anne Bamford (2006) notes that global connectivity has seen dominant policies and practices create similar histories of art education in countries around the world. International programmes such as the *International Baccalaureate* are often world leaders, with many national curricula drawing inspiration from, or copying, their programmes. This sets a standard for quality, and also allows students to more easily move between schools, even if they move to another country (Bamford, 2006: 30). Thus, some observations gleaned from examining arts education policies in Australia, the UK and the United States may have wider implications.

However, it is also worth noting that such internationalization may come at the expense of local and contextual considerations. In current national art curricula documentation, we see an increasing reference to arts education playing a role in students' learning about their national identity and local cultural identities. This is particularly vital in relation to colonized lands and in reference to indigenous cultures such as the Australian Aborigines and the Māori and Pasifika peoples of Aotearoa New Zealand, whose knowledge and traditions have for too long been usurped by white Europeans. Thus, it will not come as a surprise that there is much variance in practice, at the local, regional and international levels, even where we find detailed national arts programmes of study with specific aims and clear objectives.

It is also worth distinguishing between education *in* the arts and education *through* the arts. Bamford (2006: 70) identifies 'a clear distinction between education in the arts and education through the arts. These should be considered in a complementary but separate manner when considering arts education policy and practices.' Education in the arts is a form of dedicated arts learning, whereas integrated arts learning is education through the arts. Education through the arts, or integrated arts pedagogies are when artistic media and techniques are utilized in the service of another lesson or subject, or even as a playful activity designed to take up time or offer a respite from other (usually academic) subjects. An example of education through the arts is when the assessment for a history lesson may be to write a story, but creative writing is not the goal here; rather, the goal is to learn about and memorize some historical event. The former, education in the arts, prioritizes learning about art and is more common in secondary schools, whereas the latter is often seen in primary schools, where various subjects are taught using artistic and creative media and pedagogies. Often, but not always, this also correlates to the fact that it is more likely that a specialist arts educator will teach dedicated arts classes at secondary school level and generalist teachers (who teach other subjects and are not usually trained specifically in art) teach art at primary school level. The arguments in this book will focus on education in the arts in the form of dedicated arts classes, but occasionally reference will be made to education through the arts.

What will become apparent is that, despite the nuanced and academically rigorous arts education curricula, the reality of which schools and students have access to good-quality arts education is much less consistent. There are inequitable distributions of time, effort, space and resources across primary and secondary schools that unfairly disadvantage the eldest students in the final years of mandatory schooling when focus on academic achievement intensifies, the poorest students, students from ethnic minorities and low socio-economic geographical areas. In general there is poor resourcing for arts subjects, particularly in comparison to other subject areas and especially when compared to the STEM subjects which are prioritized along with English, as evidenced by the importance placed on literacy and numeracy. The exception to this is often fee-paying, well-regarded private schools including performing art schools which can afford excellent resources and qualified arts teachers. Meanwhile, those students who arguably most need access to the arts are often the ones missing out.

Arts education policies

The justification for teaching the various arts to school-aged pupils in the developed Western world seems to be in part historical or habitual: they have always been taught and a good understanding of society's cultural contributions seems important from a historical and nationalistic perspective. Increasingly, indigenous art has also been mentioned as worthy of engagement and a positive way to better understand the indigenous cultures in colonized lands. Teaching the arts is also thought to be a constructive and creative form of self-expression which, for children developing their sense of personal identity and seeking to understand their position in the world, means channelling their thoughts and feelings into movement, music or paint. Perhaps what is implicit is the hope that such artistic expression will alleviate frustrated outbursts that may otherwise result in the destruction of property, illegal graffiti or fist fights – but this is never explicitly stated, of course.

The policy documents detailing the national arts curriculum in Australia refer to all primary and secondary students in Australia being entitled to quality educational experiences in dance, drama, media arts, music and the visual arts because of their

> capacity to engage, inspire and enrich all students, exciting the imagination and encouraging them to reach their creative and expressive potential. The five arts subjects in the Australian Curriculum provide opportunities for students to learn how to create, design, represent, communicate and share their imagined and conceptual ideas, emotions, observations and experiences.

The aims of the national arts curriculum are to develop students':

- creativity, critical thinking, aesthetic knowledge and understanding about arts practices, through making and responding to artworks with increasing self-confidence

- arts knowledge and skills to communicate ideas; they value and share their arts and life experiences by representing, expressing and communicating ideas, imagination and observations about their individual and collective worlds to others in meaningful ways
- use of innovative arts practices with available and emerging technologies, to express and represent ideas, while displaying empathy for multiple viewpoints
- understanding of Australia's histories and traditions through the arts, engaging with the artworks and practices, both traditional and contemporary, of Aboriginal and Torres Strait Islander Peoples
- understanding of local, regional and global cultures, and their arts histories and traditions, through engaging with the worlds of artists, artworks, audiences and arts professions.

(Australian Curriculum Assessment and Reporting Authority, 2014)

Australia's national curriculum is implemented by education departments in each state and territory (i.e. Australian Capital Territory, New South Wales, Northern Territory, Queensland, South Australia, Tasmania, Victoria and Western Australia).

We see in the relevant Australian policy document that the justification for teaching students dance, drama, media arts, music and the visual arts is tied to the development of personal skills such as self-expression, self-confidence, empathy and perspective taking, developing the use of one's imagination, and the skills of observation. There is also an emphasis on the connection between learning about art in schools and developing an understanding of local history and cultures – particularly the local indigenous cultures – with a focus on the ways in which local, regional and global cultures have been expressed in artful ways. The knowledge associated with the arts and arts education is that of art techniques, art forms and media, which includes understanding and analysis of the formal features of art – what are called the elements and principles of art in the final examinations (i.e. SCSA, 2019). Examined knowledge also includes knowing about specific artists, art history, and having an awareness of the social, cultural and historical contexts that impact upon art in terms of both its creation and its reception.

In the UK, the current National Curriculum in England has been in operation since 2014 with a strong focus on maths and English from key stage 1 (lower primary school, years 1 and 2, in which children are aged between five and seven years). Art and design and music are also mandatory subjects. The Department for Education (DfE) explains the purpose of the art and design programme of study in terms similar to those used in the Australian curriculum. There is reference to creativity, critical thinking, the country's cultural history and technical skills:

> Art, craft and design embody some of the highest forms of human creativity. A high-quality art and design education should engage, inspire and challenge pupils, equipping them with the knowledge and skills to experiment, invent and create their own works of art, craft and design. As pupils progress, they should be able to think critically and develop a more rigorous understanding of art and design. They should also know how art and design both reflect and shape our history, and contribute to the culture, creativity and wealth of our nation.
>
> (DfE, 2013a)

There is the expectation that primary school-aged students in the UK learn a range of art and design practices, including the use of drawing, painting and sculpture; using colour, pattern, texture and shape; and observing artworks from a range of artists and designers. At secondary level, proficiency in using a range of artistic materials and techniques is developed, along with the ability to evaluate students' own work. Also included for older pupils is the study of the history of art, craft and design. The aims of England's national curriculum for art and design are for pupils to:

- produce creative work, exploring their ideas and recording their experiences
- become proficient in drawing, painting, sculpture and other art, craft and design techniques
- evaluate and analyse creative works using the language of art, craft and design
- know about great artists, craft makers and designers, and understand the historical and cultural development of their art forms.

(DfE, 2013a)

England's music curriculum refers to the study of music as a way to develop students' personal qualities and attitudes as well as their musical knowledge. There is reference to creativity, self-confidence and listening with discrimination. The purpose of the mandatory music programmes of study is described as follows:

> Music is a universal language that embodies one of the highest forms of creativity. A high-quality music education should engage and inspire pupils to develop a

love of music and their talent as musicians, and so increase their self-confidence, creativity and sense of achievement. As pupils progress, they should develop a critical engagement with music, allowing them to compose, and to listen with discrimination to the best in the musical canon.

And the aims of the national curriculum for music are that all pupils:

- perform, listen to, review and evaluate music across a range of historical periods, genres, styles and traditions, including the works of the great composers and musicians
- learn to sing and to use their voices, to create and compose music on their own and with others, have the opportunity to learn a musical instrument, use technology appropriately and have the opportunity to progress to the next level of musical excellence
- understand and explore how music is created, produced and communicated, including through the interrelated dimensions: pitch, duration, dynamics, tempo, timbre, texture, structure and appropriate musical notations.

(DfE, 2013b)

The knowledge associated with music that is assessable is connected to specific skills to do with musical performance, appreciation, music history and critical analysis. As we can see, the national arts curricula in the UK (particularly in England) and in Australia are similar and they, generally speaking, emphasize the arts as valuable – focussing on the technical skills, personal attributes such as self-expression, creativity and imagination, and historical and cultural appreciation that are developed when studying the arts.

In the United States of America there is not the same unified approach to arts education in policy terms as we have witnessed in the form of Australia or England's national curriculum. Public education falls under the jurisdiction of the states and counties in the United States, 'so there are many differences in how the arts are conceptualised, understood, practised and experienced in educational curricula and in schools' (O'Neill & Schmidt, 2017: 187). Taking California as an example (as one of the largest and most populated states in the United States), the subject areas on the state school curriculum include health, history and social science, mathematics, physical education, English language arts, science, visual and performing arts and world languages. The curriculum framework for visual and performing arts details the 'skills, knowledge, and abilities in dance, music, theatre, and the visual arts that all students should be able to master from prekindergarten to grade 12' (California State Board of Education, 2004).

In the foreword to this current guiding policy document, the opening justification for arts education is summed up as follows, 'one of our jobs as educators is to nurture our students' creativity and knowledge' (*ibid,* vi). The programme focusses on five aspects: 'artistic perception; creative expression; historical and cultural context; aesthetic valuing; and connections, relationships, and applications' (*ibid,* vi) in relation to dance, music, theatre and the visual arts. It is specifically noted that media and technology are included in this framework and an appeal is also made to the vocational and economic viability of studying the arts. This is due to the fact that 'California is an international leader in the technology and entertainment industries; providing our students with an education in the arts supports our state's future and our economy' (*ibid,* vi).

In terms of the aims and outcomes of California's visual and performing arts programme, these are listed according to the five aspects noted above:

Students in a comprehensive programme are expected to master the standards of an arts discipline, which are grouped under the following strands:

A. Artistic perception refers to processing, analyzing, and responding to sensory information through the use of the language and skills unique to dance, music, theatre, and the visual arts.
B. Creative expression involves creating a work, performing, and participating in the arts disciplines. Students apply processes and skills in composing, arranging, and performing a work and use a variety of means to communicate meaning and intent in their own original formal and informal works.
C. Historical and cultural context concerns the work students do toward understanding the historical contributions and cultural dimensions of an arts discipline. Students analyze roles, functions, development in the discipline, and human diversity as it relates to that discipline. They also examine closely musicians, composers, artists, writers, actors, dancers, and choreographers as well as cultures and historical periods.
D. Aesthetic valuing includes analyzing and critiquing works of dance, music, theatre, and the visual arts. Students apply processes and skills to productions or performances. They also critically assess and derive meaning from the work of a discipline, including their own, and from performances and original works based on the elements and principles of an arts discipline, aesthetic qualities, and human responses.
E. Connections, relationships, and applications involve connecting and applying what is learned in one arts discipline and comparing it to learning in the other arts, other subject areas, and careers. Students develop competencies and creative skills in problem solving, communication, and

time management that contribute to lifelong learning, including career skills. They also learn about careers in and related to arts disciplines.
(California State Board of Education, 2004: 3)

Taking the example of arts education in California, we see some similar justifications used to support arts education in America as were evident in the Australian and English curricula. Familiar themes include students' creative expression, the skills of interpretation and analysis of artworks, and a sensitivity to historical and cultural contexts in which artworks are produced and displayed. What is noticeable in the American context, however, is a stronger emphasis on the vocational aspect of studying the arts with a focus on 'connections and relationships' which sounds decidedly corporate.

This language of networking may be explained by two features of arts education in the United States. Firstly, schools across America increasingly seek to establish partnerships with local community groups, such as cultural organizations and institutions, which supplement the provision of arts education in their local areas. Examples include collective enterprises such as Houston's Arts Access Initiative, Boston's Arts Expansion Initiative, Chicago's Creative Schools Initiative and Seattle's Creative Advantage (Kisida & Bowen, 2019). This encourages constructive community relationships to be established with connections between schools and local artists and businesspeople. Not only do such school-community partnerships support local community groups and artists, they also offer students access to the expertise of skilled arts practitioners. This is coupled with the vocational emphasis evident on educational curricula. For example, the Californian visual and performing arts curriculum notes the role the arts play in preparing students for careers as well as full participation in society, stating, 'arts education provides direct training for jobs in the flourishing arts industry in California' (California State Board of Education, 2004: 4). And, 'further, education in the arts prepares students for work in any field' (*ibid*, 5). This vocational justification for studying the arts is notable and particularly interesting in the context of California, a state in the United States with a thriving International arts industry.

Arts education in practice

Despite arts education being included and, increasingly, compulsory on educational curricula in recent years, there are gaps between policy and practice. There are obvious distinctions between the stated entitlement of all children to enjoy good arts education throughout their schooling years, and the lived experience of students in terms of the quality and access they have to study arts subjects. Australia, the UK and many states in the United States all mandate arts education as a requirement for school-aged students, yet not all students get much time or resources devoted to arts education, particularly in comparison to their other timetabled subjects. The arts are simply not viewed as being as academically rigorous or educationally necessary as other subjects such as mathematics, English (which is increasingly narrowly interpreted to include literacy, spelling, punctuation and grammar), science and technology (so-called STEM subjects).

The arts are often viewed as a 'soft' option, despite the movement towards discipline-based art education (DBAE), formulated by the J. Paul Getty Trust Foundation in the 1980s in the United States. This now dominant model for teaching the arts sought to bring the arts into line with existing academic subjects in terms of including requisite testable knowledge, standards and a framework suitable for *all* students, not just those who were artistic or talented. Yet, particularly as students enter upper secondary school, the focus – of the school, the students and their parents and guardians – turns to those examinable 'STEM' subjects whose results count disproportionately or exclusively towards end of school rankings and university entrance examinations.

National testing on literacy and numeracy is increasingly evaluated at ever-younger year levels, and the results determine school and student rankings and carry significance in terms of parental choice of school, fiscal allocations and teacher hires. As such, we see even younger primary school-aged students having their arts education provisions cut to redirect time and resources into those subjects (i.e. maths and English) that are measured. Furthermore, what these developed Western countries (and others) have in common is that arts education and the quality of teaching and resources, much like that of educational provision in general, vary according to socio-economic demographics, geographical areas and whether the school is public (state- or publicly-funded) or independent/private (often referred to as 'public' in the UK). Generally, disadvantaged students[1] attend public schools, which are the schools that suffer the most from funding cuts, and therefore it is these students who will have less access to good quality arts education. And this is on top of the fact that, more generally, the arts suffer even more in comparison to their 'more academic' counterparts in schools that cater to such demographics.

Arts education in the United States of America

Educational provisions in America are organized at the regional level by states and counties. These state departments establish their policies, educational curricula and guiding documents. Most states mandate arts education as compulsory for all students. For instance, as Bamford (2006: 67) notes, arts education in the United States is 'listed as a core academic subject in the *No Child Left Behind Act (2002),* which is the reauthorization of the *Elementary and Secondary Education Act of 1965* and is included as part of education policy'. However, many children in American schools receive little to no formal arts education as a part of the curriculum. Such assertions are the conclusions of up-to-date, widespread empirical research, with the American Academy of Arts & Sciences (2021) claiming:

> In the 20 years since the *No Child Left Behind Act of 2001* defined 'arts' as a 'core academic subject', and the six years since the *Every Student Succeeds Act* declared them as part of a 'well-rounded education', arts education in American public schools has shrunk dramatically. The Commission on the Arts,[2] at the American Academy of Arts & Sciences, says we are at a crisis point, where access to arts education is declining steadily – and action must be taken to reverse the trend.

Bamford (2006: 67) noted that 'the most recent survey report, *Arts Education in Public Elementary and Secondary Schools: 1999–2000* found that provisions were dispersed and sporadic' and since then, the situation has declined even further. In order to investigate such claims in more detail, we will now consider the provision of arts education in a single state in the United States.

New York State Education Law mandates that all students in grades 7–12 receive core arts instruction from certified teachers. The Office of the New York City Comptroller conducted a survey of all the schools in New York City recording how many fulltime, part-time and casual certified arts teachers they had, how many dedicated arts rooms, and whether they had any existing arts and cultural partnerships (McGill, Eckstein & Stringer, 2014). What they discovered was that the provision of arts education in the state schools across New York City is both inequitable and underfunded. Further statistics from the New York City Department of Education's Annual Arts in Schools Reports show steep declines in spending on the arts – including on teachers, arts and cultural organizations, arts supplies and equipment – over the past seven years (McGill, Eckstein & Stringer, 2014). There was also the accusation and evidence provided that these schools have had access to specific funding for arts education, yet many of the schools instead used these funds on other, non-arts related costs. The Executive Summary of the report notes its findings as follows:

- 419 schools in New York City (28 percent) lack even one full-time, certified arts teacher, including 20 percent of all high schools (76), 22 percent of all middle schools (59) and 38 percent of all elementary schools (232);
- 306 schools (20 per cent) have neither a full – nor a part-time certified arts teacher, including 14 percent of all high schools (53), 13 percent of all middle schools (34) and 30 percent of all elementary schools (182); and
- 16 percent of schools have no arts or cultural partnerships and 10 percent of schools have no dedicated arts room.

Furthermore, it is clear that reductions in arts education have fallen disproportionately on the City's lower income neighbourhoods, especially the South Bronx and Central Brooklyn. While these two neighbourhoods are home to just 31 percent of all City schools, this report found that:

- More than 42 percent of schools that lack either full-time or part-time certified arts teachers are located in the South Bronx and Central Brooklyn; and
- Nearly half of the schools that lack both a certified arts teacher and an arts or cultural partnership are located in the South Bronx and Central Brooklyn.

(McGill, Eckstein & Stringer, 2014: 1)

Such findings are troubling, particularly when the situation in New York City is not an anomaly. A few years earlier, between 2008 and 2010, at the time of President Obama's explicit support for the arts, the President's Committee on the Arts and Humanities (PCAH) conducted a survey into the state of arts education across America. They produced a report that also evidenced variation in the arts offerings and uptake amongst school-aged students in different geographical locations. The executive summary (PCAH, 2011) notes:

> While we found a growing body of research to support positive educational outcomes associated with arts-rich schools, and many schools and programs engaged in such work, we also found enormous variety in the delivery of arts education, resulting in a complex patchwork with pockets of visionary activity flourishing in some locations and inequities in access to arts education increasing in others.

The PCAH were keen to explore opportunities and detail recommendations for the ways in which arts education may assist with issues such as the persistently high school dropout rates in the United States and the inequalities associated with educational provision, particularly for those from non-white and lower socio-economic backgrounds. The report notes that 'increased academic achievement, school engagement, and creative thinking' are outcomes positively associated with arts education (PCAH, 2011: vi) and 'arts integration models, the practice of teaching across classroom subjects in tandem with the arts, have been yielding some particularly promising results in school reform and closing the achievement gap' (PCAH, 2011: vi).

Yet, even while recognizing the benefits of teaching in and through the arts, it was noted that arts education is 'on a downward trend' (PCAH, 2011: vi) due to budget cuts and a focus on subjects that are tested with a view to increase school rankings – subjects that typically count towards university entrance exam scores and that are well perceived by prospective employers. The five recommendations made in the report include encouraging collaborations between arts educators, professional associations and artists, and federal and state agencies; expanding arts integration with more professional development for classroom teachers; and expanding in-school opportunities for teaching artists (PCAH, 2011: vii). They also identified 'the need for federal and state education leaders to provide policy guidance for employing the arts to increase the rigor of curriculum, strengthen teacher quality, and improve low-performing schools' (PCAH, 2011: viii) and the desirability of gathering more evidence about arts education, including the progress of students, teacher quality, resources and equitable access to arts education.

In the foreword, Arne Duncan, US Secretary of Education at the time, stresses the vocational advantage that accompanies studying the arts. He writes that future employees will need to be creative and arts education will play an essential role 'in preparing students for success in the knowledge and innovation economy' (PCAH, 2011:1). It goes to show what the public and political rhetoric, and policy to support it, may look like when the leader of a Nation supports the arts and sees their value. In 2008 President Barack Obama created an Arts Policy Council designed to reinvest in arts education. Duncan goes on to acknowledge that:

> President Obama ... firmly believes that arts education builds innovative thinkers who will become our nation's leaders in government, business, and the nonprofit sectors. For today's students to be the innovators and economic leaders of the future, they will need to have experiences as musicians and dancers, painters and sculptors, poets and playwrights – in short, they will need to be creative innovators who will build our nation's economy for the future. They also will

sustain a rich and vibrant culture to nourish the heart and soul of the American people, and to communicate with our neighbors around the globe.

(PCAH, 2011: 3)

Unfortunately, the President's Committee on the Arts and the Humanities no longer exists. Its committee members resigned in August 2017 in protest of President Donald Trump's response to the 'Unite the Right rally' held in Charlottesville, Virginia (O'Keefe, 2017a, 2017b) and authority for the committee subsequently lapsed the following month. What effect, if any, this will have on arts education across the United States, and, more importantly, what effect the Trump Presidency term has had on educational provisions and arts education in America is yet to be ascertained.

It is clear that, in general, younger students across primary school years have the most time to spend on the arts and are more likely to be taught in an arts-integrated fashion; namely, where the arts are somehow integrated into other subjects or lessons. Students have *less* arts education as they progress through their schooling years and, by their final years of school, arts classes are usually only taken in an optional capacity as the focus of students is narrowed on to the subjects that will be examined in order for them to complete their high school certificates and university entrance exams. For instance, O'Neill and Schmidt (2017: 197) note that in America,

> some form of music or other arts education is a mandated requirement in the elementary years ... in about 45 of the 50 states in the USA. In secondary schools, however, music and arts education are typically and widely structured as electives – notwithstanding the fact that arts education is mandated in 45 states, only 26 require any arts coursework for high school graduation.

The stereotype of arts subjects as 'soft', or not as academically rigorous as, say, mathematics, English or science, is perpetuated by the fact that many arts subjects are positioned and correspondingly selected as 'electives' in secondary school. In this way they become fun options that give enjoyment or light relief amidst the toil of difficult and intellectually challenging academic subjects that are assessed for secondary school leaving certificates and university entrance scores.

Arts education in Australia

The fact that teachers prioritize subjects that are tested and seen to be more academically rigorous is unsurprising. However, these trends start early with the timetable and teachers' focus reflecting this bias from primary school. As reported by Gibson and Anderson (2008: 107), the arts in Australian state schools are still marginalized, and '[t]he desire "to promote the value of the arts as a lifelong learning choice for every Australian" (Australia Council for the Arts, 2002: 131) becomes little more than rhetoric'. They also point out the gap between policy and practice, noting the 'large gap between the espoused policy in arts education and existing provisions within classrooms' (Gibson & Anderson, 2008: 107), which sees approximately 25–35 per cent of time in the primary classroom spent on English, 20 per cent on mathematics and only 6–10 per cent spent on the creative and practical arts. This translates to twenty-five to thirty minutes per week spent on arts education in Australian primary schools.

In secondary schools, Gibson and Anderson note that it is harder to determine how much time is spent on arts subjects. They explain that, for example, '[w]hile music and visual arts are mandatory in Years 7 and 8 of New South Wales secondary schools, drama and dance are often not offered at this level; and if they are, they are offered as curriculum options for students' (2008: 108). Again, as was the case in the United States, we see the offering of some arts subjects moving from mandatory at the primary school level to elective at the secondary school level in Australian state schools as the focus shifts to more academic or testable subjects.

One obvious factor driving these subject priorities in Australia is the existence of the *National Assessment Program – Literacy and Numeracy (NAPLAN)*. NAPLAN is an annual national assessment for students in Years 3, 5, 7 and 9 that tests four domains: reading, writing, language conventions (spelling, grammar and punctuation) and numeracy. These results inform students' and school rankings and place a competitive urgency on maths and English. These priorities are echoed in the availability of professional development opportunities for teachers, with a clear focus on improving NAPLAN test results. As a result, professional development on arts subjects for teachers suffers, missing out because schools' strategic goals are to improve their NAPLAN test results and overall school rankings. As teacher training and ongoing professional development support are directed at increasing students' literacy and numeracy scores so as to improve school rankings, professional learning in the arts is simply not a priority, as Chapman et al. (2018: 21) note with respect to primary schools in Western Australia. They point out this 'is a result of the emphasis on standardized testing and schools responding to that situation and teachers are required to participate in these focused activities' (Chapman et al., 2018: 21). We can only conclude that this lack of focus on the arts directly correlates to testing and outcomes such as the essential NAPLAN testing and attendant league tables in Australia.

Arguably, the Australian government's focus on issues other than arts education has also translated into the (lack of) funding opportunities for research in this field. There is a need for more research to be conducted on arts education, and, certainly, the dearth of Australian research into arts education has not gone unnoticed. Gibson and Anderson (2008: 105) comment on the shocking lack of studies commissioned in Australia, noting, 'In 2004, the Australia Council for Educational Research (ACER) was commissioned by the Australian Government to write an *Evaluation of School-based Arts Education Programmes in Australian Schools*. Not surprisingly, this research found only four relevant Australian studies.' They continue by arguing that

> the recent ACER report into school-based arts education programmes in Australian schools indicates that this is an opportune time to engage in significant, longitudinal research that will supply hard-edged evidence on the impact of arts education programmes on student outcomes, both academic and social.
>
> (Gibson & Anderson, 2008: 110)

The message is loud and clear: there is a worry that Australia is falling behind the UK and the United States in terms of the research conducted and published on arts education and more work is desperately needed in this area.

What the existing research demonstrates is that it is certainly the case that the practice of arts education across schools throughout Australia does not consistently offer what is promised in the national policy, with the failure to meet this standard most obvious in state schools in lower socio-economic areas. Robyn Ewing (2020: 79) sums up the problem of the gap between policy and practice when she notes:

> While the rhetoric values the place of the Arts in the Australian curriculum, for *The Curriculum: The Arts* to be actioned effectively, there would need to be much resourcing, teacher professional learning and prioritising of the Arts in schools. Many contemporary school settings remain devoid of quality arts resources and the challenge of access for some children continues.

As we have already seen, such educational priorities are replicated in America. '[In the] United States, Conway et al. (2005) noted that most professional learning was steered toward traditional academic subjects and that arts teachers' professional learning needs are rarely considered' (Chapman et al., 2018: 21). Such concerns to do with the lack of support for arts educators extend to other resources, including designated arts rooms, materials and access to good-quality artworks. This is also the case in the UK, where the lack of good quality arts resources has been bemoaned with calls for the government to provide a 'level playing field' in terms of schools, students and teachers' access to visual art. Recently, the head of the Tate art galleries complained about the fact that hardworking teachers struggle, only to be 'thwarted' in their attempts to provide an arts-rich education due to the 'dire lack of resources' at their disposal (Gibbons, 2019). Therefore, we see arts education policy wording in Australia, the UK and the United States as positively explaining why arts education is compulsory, but unless proper resources and support are provided to teachers, quality arts education is threatened.

Arts education in the UK

We have seen that even where national education curricula include a compulsory role for arts education across all schooling years and even where arts education policies positively proclaim the benefits of education in the arts, corresponding educational experiences are not of a consistently high quality. Similar observations may also be made of the role the arts play in society more generally. Despite political rhetoric about the importance of the arts, in recent years there has been a downward spiral in terms of funding for the arts, including for arts education, coupled with fewer employment opportunities for arts educators or chances to collaborate with arts organizations and creative industries. Although it is unknown to what extent one causes the other, there is a corresponding decline in the number of students opting to study the arts in recent years.

In its *Changing Lives: The social impact of participation in culture and sport* report from 2019, the UK government's department for Culture, Media and Sport paints a rosy picture of the richness of the UK's cultural offerings. The nation boasts (at least) '40,000 community choirs, 11,000 amateur orchestras, 50,000 amateur arts groups, 5,000 amateur theatre societies, 3,000 dance groups, 2,500 museums, 400 historic places, 4,000 libraries, 1,300 theatres and 50,000 book clubs'. Positively, in 2017–18, the majority of adults in England engaged with the arts in some form or another, including visiting heritage sites, museums and art galleries. Yet the report also notes that the level of cultural participation is not increasing and has not increased over the past five years and, additionally, there remains a disproportionate and uneven distribution of those who engage with the arts as variations are noted in terms of gender, ethnicity, disability, age, socioeconomic group and geographical location. The concern is that the arts are inaccessible to some and thus are seen to be – and actually remain – elitist.

This report follows from the same department's 2016 *Culture White Paper*, in which the UK government reinforced the fact that their national educational programmes are designed to ensure that all students study art and design, music, drama, dance and design and technology, from primary school all the way up to the final examinable school year levels (GCSE and A levels). While the statistics demonstrated that the majority of children do engage with the arts in some way (in 2017–18 '96 per cent of children in England aged 5–15 engaged with the arts, either in or out of school'), there were 'significant variations in the type of activity and whether children were able to participate at school' (UK govt, 2016; UK govt, 2019). Despite the many wonderful cultural activities available within the UK, despite the surveys reporting that the majority of people living in the UK value the arts and deem them to be an enjoyable and important aspect of life, and also despite the fact that the arts are a requirement on the national curriculum, arts subjects in schools do not receive the time and attention they deserve. The *Changing Lives* report (UK govt, 2019) notes the decline in arts education in the UK, concluding that:

> 62. There was widespread concern in the evidence that we received about changes to the school curriculum leading to a decline in arts education from early years, through primary and into secondary education.

[and]

> 74. We are deeply concerned by the evidence we received around the downgrading of arts subjects in schools, with all the consequent implications for children's development, wellbeing, experiences, careers and, ultimately, life chances.

Furthermore, this report also drew upon empirical research to detail the fact that, over the past decade, numbers of student enrolments in specialized arts subjects have decreased. It is also the case that less specialist arts teachers are employed by schools across the UK. The report sums up some of these statistics as follows:

> 64. The Cultural Learning Alliance estimated that the take up of arts GCSE courses had reduced by 28% since 2010, that there had been a 17% decline in arts subject teaching time and a 16% reduction in specialist secondary school teachers. Similar concerns have recently been raised by Ofsted, citing evidence that secondary school pupils are dropping arts subjects before reaching their GCSE years.

[and]

66. Furthermore, the numbers of music teachers had also fallen year on year, with the average numbers of music staff in independent schools much higher than in state schools. Of the responding schools [500 schools in England who participated in a survey conducted by the University of Sussex], 18% offered no GCSE music option at all and the decline is set to continue. Those offering music at 'A' level also fell by 15.4% between 2016 and 2018, with further falls expected, and numbers offering 'A' level Music Technology declined by 31.7%.

(UK govt, 2019)

Such declines in the provision and uptake of arts education across the UK simply do not match the political rhetoric and educational policies that promote the value of teaching the arts to all school students. What arts education looks like 'in practice' is a mismatch to the policies that dictate the compulsory nature of education in art and design, music, drama, dance and design and technology, throughout the schooling years.

The decline in arts education in the UK has been significant enough to be reported in the news. For example, Hill (2018) notes that registrations for arts GCSEs in England have steadily decreased over the past six years:

Registrations for 2018 arts GCSEs in England have plummeted by a further 51,000, taking the total fall in entries to almost 150,000 over the past five years. New data published by qualifications regulator Ofqual show that since 2014, arts subjects have seen a 25.6% fall in entries. Over the same period, total GCSE entries have grown by 3.4% … Arts subjects now account for just 1 in 12 of all GCSEs taken, compared with around 1 in 8 five years ago. The GCSE subjects showing the strongest growth are exclusively those included in the English Baccalaureate (EBacc) – the suite of subjects included in the Government's performance measure for schools. While the take-up of EBacc subjects has grown by 5% this year, at the same time there has been a 13% fall in entries for non-EBacc subjects.

The decreased attention given to arts subjects and the declining number of student enrolments in specialist arts subjects can be directly linked to which subjects are valued. Schools, and students along with their parents and guardians, are likely to focus on academic subjects that they believe will be most valued by universities (when pupils leave compulsory schooling and seek further education opportunities) and future employers. Increasingly, such subjects include English, mathematics, science, geography, history and languages, which together comprise the English Baccalaureate; subjects that universities favour when assessing student applications. Thus, these are also subjects parents prioritize as 'academic' and schools prioritize them also given the resulting scores are counted in school league tables.

Such a selection immediately narrows the focus of schools, students, parents and the government if it is only this handful of subjects to which they are attending when taking into account grades in order to determine academic ability, rankings and placements. Worryingly, this narrow focus is getting even narrower as the EBacc is being phased out due to a lack of interest in the study of languages. Just recently, TES (2022) reports that the 'lack of students taking language GCSEs will lead to the government's flagship English Baccalaureate targets being "quietly phased out". This is because there are insufficient numbers of students willing to study a modern language for the EBacc criteria to be met.

If results and outcomes are deemed to be the main aim of schooling, then of course students – presumably guided by appropriate adults – will choose to enrol in academic subjects in which good results afford them further academic and vocational opportunities. As such, diminished attention is paid to other subjects, including the arts, which have no role to play in this reductive calculation. Echoing these concerning figures, Rosen (2019) laments this narrowing approach to education that sees less students studying the arts. Rosen (2019) explains the decline in students taking English Literature, music and drama GSCEs as follows, 'One reason for this is that schools are judged on their success in getting students to achieve success at Ebacc – a raft of five GCSEs, which exclude arts subjects'. Accordingly, less students enrol in the arts and less specialist teachers are employed to teach them. That this is the case in the UK is manifest in the empirical data.

These claims are further evidenced by the fact that the numbers of arts teachers being employed in the UK are also on a downward trajectory. It is reported that 9,000 art teachers employed in English secondary schools have left their jobs since 2011 (Knott, 2018) and these jobs have simply not been replaced. The figures cited from records kept by the Department for Education demonstrate that schools are employing less arts teachers (a fall of 22 per cent from 2011 to 2018) and the loss of arts teachers is double that of overall teacher numbers. Knott (2018) writes:

> There were 41,300 teachers of arts subjects for pupils in year groups 7 to 13 in the country's state schools in 2011, according to figures published by the Department for Education (DfE) last week. But this number had fallen to 32,300 by last year.

> The largest fall has been in the number of drama teachers, which has dropped by 2,600 (22%), from 11,600 to 9,000. The number of art and design teachers has fallen by 2,100 (15%) from its level of 13,900 in 2011, and there are 1,500 (19%) fewer music teachers.
>
> [Furthermore:]
>
> The biggest fall in teacher numbers has been in those teaching at GCSE level. There were 5,100 fewer arts subject teachers of years 10 and 11 (key stage 4) in 2018 than in 2011 – a reduction of 20%.
>
> The figures are likely to fuel concern that arts subjects are being marginalised because they are not part of the English Baccalaureate (EBacc) – the suite of subjects used by the Government to assess school performance. The number of pupils studying GCSEs in arts subjects has fallen by 26% since 2014, according to figures published earlier this year by the qualifications regulator Ofqual.
>
> (Knott, 2018)

Phillips (2019) concurs with the conclusion drawn above, noting that the general perception seems to be that the creative arts are not simply valuable – and by that what is most specifically meant is that the arts are not economically viable given the lack of employability options that results from their pursuit. If the government needs to tighten its belt, the first thing that is cut is funding to the arts – both within society and in arts education. Phillips (2019) draws a direct causal line between governments reducing their expenditure and 'major reductions in what art schools have to spend per pupil, directly affecting the extent and quality of the country's arts and design courses'. Thus, the connection between arts education policies, the experience of students studying arts subjects in schools, and the government's political interests and budget expenditure seems to be inextricably linked. This conclusion is reiterated in the most recent review of the arts in UK schools, as demonstrated by this quote from the executive summary of *The Arts in Schools: Foundations for the Future* (Tambling & Bacon, 2023: 8):

> Since the National Curriculum was introduced there have been multiple changes of direction and little focus on the purposes of education. There is no systemic rationale for what is taught, and no coherent and ambitious vision for education in relation to the economy, society, community or the individual: as a result, we have a schooling system that prioritises school performance based on exam grades in defined subject areas, and in which success measures do not value the whole child. In the absence of consensus around purpose, in the context of increased accountability focused on a narrow range of subject areas, and acute funding pressures, there has been a systematic downgrading or exclusion of arts subjects and experiences.

Structural barriers have led to a lack of subject parity. At every stage in the schooling system the arts are disadvantaged: at initial teacher recruitment and training through to a lack of support for arts teaching in primary schools. The prioritisation of EBacc (non-arts) subjects in secondary accountability measures has meant a reduction in the level of arts subjects, teachers and resources available, and therefore declining GCSE and A Level take-up. Dance and drama have no parity at inspection level, and film and digital media have been excluded from the national curriculum. We have an assessment regime that does not work for arts subjects, which require different kinds of measurement, and the investment required to develop these has not been made because of their perceived low status. Finally, we have the long tail of the exclusion of the arts from the higher education facilitating subjects list before 2019, thereby further disincentivising arts take-up. Loss of subjects and teachers cannot easily be reversed. This downgrading of the arts is damaging for young people's lives and aspirations, for the arts education workforce, for the workforce more widely, and for the health and diversity of the creative industries. And access to the arts is not equitable: we have a two-tier system, with the arts more highly valued in independent schools.

These worrying trends in schooling and the resulting negative impact upon the arts and aesthetic education are evident across all of the developed Western countries we have examined here.

Conclusion

Empirical research across multiple countries reflects similar trends and concerns in arts education. Noticeably, there is a gap between policy and practice, with a few general features. Namely, that arts education is comparatively poorly resourced, especially compared to other areas of general education, and, despite this, motivated, creative arts teachers are often able to compensate for a lack of resources in order to offer a quality arts educational experience (Bamford, 2006: 73). However, it is also reported that the teachers who teach arts subjects are a combination of general teachers, arts educators, specialist educators, artists and members of the community. Bamford (2006: 75) summarizes the fact that 'of the 46% of arts education, which is delivered by teachers, 85% are generalist teachers, i.e. teachers who teach a variety of subjects. This is particularly the case in the primary school, where the number of specialist teachers is relatively low'. As such, arts teachers have varying skills and different artistic abilities.

Furthermore, arts teachers rarely receive any specialist arts education training and the professional development opportunities are scarce. And, finally, artists and the community are playing an increasing role in the provision of arts education in schools (Bamford, 2006: 74). These general trends in arts education globally are worth noting. There is a hope that directing attention to the gap between arts education policies and corresponding national curricula which espouse the benefits of learning the arts and their manifestation in practice may lead to more equitable provision of arts education for all students.

However, supporters of the arts must also work hard to alter existing associations that present studying arts subjects as a less than favourable option for students. There seems to be a general perception of the arts as 'soft' or less academically rigorous than their more often tested and measured counterparts such as English, mathematics and science. There is also the prevalent idea that the arts are a less viable vocational choice for students, with the stereotype of the 'starving' or 'out of work' artist looming large in the cultural imagination. And yet it is simply not the case that the arts and cultural industries are not contributing to the economies of these countries. Government figures in the UK illustrate that the creative industries are in fact one of the fastest growing sectors and contribute to the economy, including by accounting for approximately 9 per cent of the UK's total exports. The Arts Council England (2019: 2) adds that in '2017 the creative industries were worth £101.5bn to the UK economy (up from £94.8bn in 2016), making it one of the fastest growing sectors, with growth at twice the average UK rate since 2010. As such, the sector offers substantial (and growing) opportunities for experience of and entry to the world of work.' Furthermore, according to the Creative Industries Federation, 35 per cent of creative workers are self-employed (Phillips, 2019).

It is the case that the wider social climate and attitudes towards the arts affect the provision and uptake of arts subjects in schools. Political decisions, particularly to do with finances and restructuring, have a direct effect on arts education. For example, as Ewing (2020: 80) notes in relation to Australia, 'funding cuts to small – and middle-sized arts organisations continue to jeopardise their future. It remains difficult to envision that the implementation of the Arts Curriculum will be prioritised or suitably resourced in the current climate.' The message that the arts are not valued is enforced when decisions are made such as that made by then Australian Prime Minister Scott Morrison in December 2019, when he announced that what was then the Department of Communications and the Arts would be rolled into a new entity called the Department of Infrastructure, Transport, Regional Development and Communications, commencing in February 2020.

This decision (made by a coalition 'Liberal' government) would mean that Australia would no longer have a national department for the arts, with the name 'arts' being dropped from the title, and this decision was made without consulting the arts department head at the time, Mike Mrdak (who has thirty-two years' experience working in the public sector) (Baker, 6th December 2019). The backlash from the arts community in Australia was swift. The director of the National Association for the Visual Arts, Esther Anatolitis, said she was 'gobsmacked' and, further criticized the government's action on the basis of not recognizing the value of the arts, including the industry's economic contribution to Australia:

> Deliberate choices have been made [here] – value choices, ideological choices. Someone has made the choice to devalue a $111.7 billion [a year] industry ... We would expect government at the highest level to reflect what makes us who we are and where we see our future as Australians. That makes this step of removing the name of the arts ministry a massive backwards step culturally for Australia.
> (Baker, 6th December 2019)

In response to this backlash, the Morrison government defended their decision, with then Minister for Communications and the Arts Paul Fletcher reassuring the arts sector that the structural change would not see any corresponding budget cuts (Baker, 11th December 2019). More recently, in July 2022, after the Australian election returned a Labor government to power after nine years of conservative rule, current prime minister Anthony Albanese renamed the department name Department of Infrastructure, Transport, Regional Development and Communications *and the Arts*, restoring the arts to the title and conveying their value.

It is important that governments acknowledge the value of the arts, and not solely in economic terms. To attempt to justify the value of the arts in financial terms is to do the arts a disservice. If the only value of education is employability, salary and how much a worker can contribute to their country's GDP, then we have gone awry, conceding defeat to the ever-narrowing terminology used to describe what is good and valuable, both educationally and in society. If the reason we use to justify arts education is that those who study the arts will be employable and thus economic contributors to society, then this reductive argument will continue to gain traction, further restricting political and public defences of the arts to the use of economic terms. These types of instrumental arguments in defence of aesthetic education will be further examined in Chapter 6, in relation to consideration of the extrinsic benefits of arts education.

As our neoliberal societies and party politics increasingly push us to describe the value of things in terms of cost-benefit analyses and use value, and consumer capitalistic trends of managerialism and standardization ensure everything must be tested and ranked, the arts suffer. They suffer as they try to reductively describe their value in these instrumental terms, and they suffer as they are pushed to the margins of society, as well as of the curriculum. When governments are seeking to cut costs, their eyes firstly fall on the arts, and secondly on education. Within education, when costs are cut, these initially disproportionally and adversely affect the arts, creating a vicious cycle in which society continually undervalues the role the arts play in contributing to the flourishing life.

With a focus on arts education, there needs to be good, sound justificatory arguments for why the arts should be taught in schools, why they should be valued and properly resourced, and why they constitute an essential component of the curriculum if we wish to educate students for flourishing lives. These flourishing lives will include having knowledge, being able to find meaningful work and earn a living, while also being able to engage critically and creatively in the political, social and cultural community of which they are a part. The arguments made must be theoretically sound, but, because we are referring to education, there must also be real-life considerations that result from the defence of arts education in schools. As such, educational policies, resources and teacher training also matter. But firstly, the existing defences for arts education must be considered and critiqued.

Given the policies and governmental agendas often spell out the importance of the arts in a well-balanced educational offering, there is room for hope. The contemporary approach to teaching the arts has been dominated since the 1980s by discipline-based art education (DBAE), which has worked to set the arts on an equal footing with other academic subjects that may be taught, assessed and learnt as a body of knowledge. While this approach has pros and cons, much like the focus of contemporary education on progress, achievement and measurement, it highlights the importance of art making, art history, art criticism and aesthetics. However, when we delve deeper, we see that the arguments used in policy and curriculum documents to defend arts education include a focus on personal qualities, such as self-expression, self-confidence, empathy and perspective taking, developing the use of one's imagination, and the skills of observation. There is also the emphasis that learning about art in schools is connected to understanding history and cultures with an emphasis on the ways in which local, regional and global cultures have been expressed in artful ways. Such defences are insufficient for our purposes, so we must critically evaluate what such arguments lack, and then consider how we can improve the defence for compulsory arts education for all school-aged pupils.

2

Why value the arts and arts education?

Introduction

Education in the arts and art theory is vital. Arts education must be supported by good educational and governmental policy, quality resourcing and teacher training in order to be practically effective. There have been those who have sought to defend arts education and aesthetic education, but more work is required in this area and on this defence. In Chapter 1 I elucidated existing policy defences for arts classes across primary and secondary levels of schooling, with a particular focus on Australia, the UK and the United States. While education in the arts is often compulsory in these and other developed countries, there are gaps between policy and practice, between the glowing reports of the benefits of arts education for school-aged children and the reality of what they experience. Most noticeably, there is a lack of appropriate resourcing, especially in public (state-funded) schools and there is an inequitable distribution of access to good-quality arts education for all students with those in lower socio-economic demographics most obviously lacking the same opportunities as elsewhere.

However, much of the policy rhetoric is positive – highlighting the importance of the arts in terms of educating students in constructive and creative means for self-expression and advocating for the historical and cultural importance of the arts. Justifications such as these are used to defend compulsory arts education across all levels of schooling throughout the world. While creative self-expression is on balance a valuable goal, and the arts do have historical and cultural significance, these are not the best defences of arts education for young people in schools. Over the next two chapters, I will explain why. In this chapter I will firstly examine and critique two well-regarded arguments that seek to defend arts education on the basis of, firstly, the role art has to play in supporting self-expression, and, secondly, a defence of the arts in relation to their role in supporting moral improvement. I will point out the weaknesses of these defences and why they will not do in light of our search for a robust justification for the necessity of compulsory aesthetic education.

Definition of terms

Allow me to clarify the terms I am using to begin with, before delving into the arguments in defence of aesthetic education. In terms of whether something (an object or a performance, for instance) may be described as a work of art, I make use of an analytical, classificatory approach to outline a definition of art that sees art as an open concept, allowing new additions to be considered as instantiations of 'art' and new art media to evolve, while not including everything in its category. Here I follow Morris Weitz (1956) in claiming that searching for a definition of art with necessary and sufficient conditions is not the best way to define art. Instead, we should make use of the Wittgensteinian notion of 'family resemblances' in order to identify whether or not something belongs to the concept because art, by its very nature, shifts and changes and artists are always pushing assumed boundaries with their creative works.

Therefore, I define art as an object that is intentionally created by a person or persons ('the artist') with the primary function or purpose of producing an aesthetic experience for those who engage with it. Such an object is created and received in a context because it is a human endeavour. For now I shall leave aside the tricky cases positioned at the edges of my definition (such as objects that may not have previously been artworks, such as cave paintings, which are now treated as art), because each instance may be judged on a case-by-case basis on this definition and I need not resolve all the controversial 'but, is it art?' examples for my theory to be considered viable.

When it comes to arts education, I use the term 'aesthetic education' because it includes theories of art alongside the skills and techniques involved in making artworks and learning how to appreciate and critique works of art. The term 'aesthetica' was first used by German philosopher Alexander Gottlieb Baumgarten (1714–62) in 1735 in his *Meditationes Philosophicae de Nonnullus ad Poema Pertinentitous.* As Collinson (1992: 178) notes in a footnote, 'he used it to refer both to sensuous knowledge and the science of the beautiful, and maintained that the aesthetic knowledge resulting from these two complemented and was as reliable as intellectual knowledge'. The term 'aesthetics' thus historically brought together the idea of the study of art and beauty as a philosophical area of research. It is to be noted that despite the (particularly historical) connection between art and beauty, the two overlapping concepts are not co-extensive (Collinson, 1992: 114). Namely, art may or may not be beautiful and that which is beautiful may or may not be an artwork. Aesthetics, as the philosophical study of art, considers key questions to do with defining and valuing art, creating, displaying and experiencing art, and art's relationship to the world.

Experiences that result from engaging with artworks are dynamic and complex. Consequently, the concept of aesthetic experience is notoriously difficult to pin down and simply refers to the experience one has, whereby the object of that experience contains aesthetic content (Shelley, 2017). As Beardsley (1982: 81) explains, a person is having an aesthetic experience 'if and only if the greater part of his [sic] mental activity during that time is united and made pleasurable by being tied to the form and qualities of a sensuously presented or imaginatively intended object on which his primary attention is concentrated'. Such aesthetic experiences are emotive as well as cognitive. They involve the intellect as well as the emotions and may be experiences of beauty, the sublime, being moved, feeling wonder or a sense of harmony and delight. Not all art objects (or indeed, all objects) may potentially produce an aesthetic experience, but neither does my account rule this out.

Classically, Frank Sibley (1965: 137) connects aesthetics with perception. Quoted by Collinson (1992: 113), Sibley draws an immediate link between the work of art and how it is experienced:

> Aesthetics deals with a kind of perception. People have to *see* the grace or unity of a work, *hear* the plaintiveness or frenzy in the music, *notice* the gaudiness of a colour scheme, *feel* the power of a novel, its mood or its uncertainty of tone … the crucial thing is to see, hear, feel.

Most aestheticians use positive superlatives in order to describe the aesthetic experience and Collinson notes such experience is highly valued:

> Aesthetic experience at its highest and best is arresting, intense and utterly engrossing; that when fully achieved it seizes one's whole mind or imagination and conveys whatever it does convey so vividly that the result is delight and knowledge.
>
> (Collinson, 1992: 115)

Yet, aesthetic experience varies widely. And often when we try to describe the experience associated with a certain object (a painting, or a dance performance, or a beautiful sunset), we quickly find ourselves describing the object of the experience itself.

In terms of defining aesthetic experience, we must do away with the idea that aesthetic experience is a unique definable *kind* of experience, as the debates between Monroe Beardsley and George Dickie have successfully proven (see Iseminger (2003) for an overview of this debate). By the 1980s, Beardsley changed his mind, from defending an internalist theory focussed on the phenomenological quality of the experience to admitting that an externalist theory, which focusses instead on the features of the object experienced, must be accurate. After all, it makes no sense to defend an aesthetic experience if the qualities of that experience are not connected to features of the object with which is being engaged. Yet listing such features is tricky given the variety of art media and accompanying experiences. Thus, most aestheticians now hold that

> an object has aesthetic value insofar as it affords valuable experience when correctly perceived. This view – which has come to be called *empiricism about aesthetic value*, given that it reduces aesthetic value to the value of aesthetic experience – has attracted many advocates over the last several years.
>
> (Shelley, 2017)

Thus, I will not be relying on a narrow formalist definition such as that defended by Clive Bell (1915) in which aesthetic experience is the provocation of particular aesthetic emotions in an appropriately sensitive person by artworks. Note, that although he is a formalist, Bell appeals to "'a peculiar … aesthetic emotion" by means of which the essential quality of works of art, "some quality common and peculiar" to them all, was to be identified. (This quality turns out to be what he called "significant form".)' (Hanfling, 1992: xii). Maxine Greene (2001: 5) also uses the term in a narrow sense, writing, '"Aesthetic," of course, is an adjective used to describe or single out the mode of experience brought into being by encounters with works of art.' Yet this seems circular, whereby engaging with artworks produces an aesthetic experience and an artwork is that which is intended to produce such an experience, and it does not allow aesthetic experience to result from engaging with nature. Rather, I am more sympathetic to the idea that aesthetic experience emerges from ordinary experience, as detailed by John Dewey.

As such, my theory is also a form of empiricism about aesthetic value and aesthetic experience is simply experience with aesthetic content, 'i.e., an experience of an object as having the aesthetic features that it has' (Shelley, 2017). In this way, I follow Beardsley in claiming that an aesthetic experience results when one's mental activity is concentrated on the 'sensuously presented or imaginatively intended object' (i.e. an artwork, performance, or natural beauty such as a sunset or lush forest or the beach) which brings pleasure to the perceiver.[1]

For an art object to produce an aesthetic experience, there are three main factors to consider: the skill with which the artist has executed the work of art, the art object itself and how it is displayed, and the attitude of the receiver of the work. Aesthetic experience depends upon an open and receptive mode of attention, but contextual features may also invoke or interrupt an aesthetic experience. If an artwork fails to elicit an aesthetic experience, this may be due to the lack of artistic skill or execution, the context in which the artwork is displayed (which may include socio-historical or ethical factors), and/or the attitude of the receiver of the artwork. Each of these elements – the skill of the artist, the presentation or display of the art object as well as the reception of the work (including, specifically, the attitude of the audience) – requires a form of learning, training or education.

The education of artists and receivers of artworks is therefore a central issue within aesthetics, which includes both practical and theoretical aspects. I will further engage with all of these concepts throughout the book. Various defences have been offered for the arts and aesthetic education, and in this chapter, I will focus on two such arguments. I shall start with the expressivist defence of art as a form of self-expression to which all people should have access, before considering whether the arts should be defended because they may support moral education. Both arguments will have educational implications.

The expressivist view of art

The first argument I shall articulate has stood the test of time (as has the view of art as imitation or a form of representation). The expressivist account of art, as articulated by Clive Bell (1915), Roger Fry (1920) and R. G. Collingwood (1938), holds that art should only seek to express and arouse distinct emotions. On this account, these aesthetes define art as 'high' art (including avant-garde artworks) because they claim it is high art, as opposed to craft or mass produced and distributed art, that may convey and therefore arouse a distinct and uniquely valuable emotional response in those who engage with it.[2] This argument may be criticized as elitist in its priority of particular kinds of artworks and art media. There is no reason to think that film, for example, cannot produce distinct emotions, although the point is taken that most formulaic rom-coms (romantic comedies) are designed to elicit a predictable feeling response, one that is recognizably different from an action movie or a thriller. Expressivists argue that high art manages to achieve distinctive emotional expression due to the refined skills of the artist who produces it and it is only upon this basis – the experience of the art and the art object itself – by which we should judge art (see Chapter 7 for a detailed critical examination of the position known as aestheticism or autonomism which relates to how aesthetes claim artworks should be judged).

Thus, we can glean that for Bell, Fry and Collingwood it is the emotional response to art that takes priority over a cognitive response (not that one has to understand feelings as the binary opposite to rationality, but certainly there exists such a historical distinction between reason and emotion). In this way, art making is a form of self-expression connected to the expression of our distinct emotions and it may follow that those engaged in this endeavour can seek to better understand and express themselves via art media. Drawing upon expressivism in defence of arts education, defenders of this position claim the reason we should include the arts, particularly art making, on the curriculum is because it is important that students learn to express themselves in various creative and constructive ways, and art media offer ways for people to do so that are unavailable in other subject areas.

The means by which we express ourselves, our ideas and emotions in other subjects such as history, mathematics and science are restricted by discipline-specific norms, and in many subjects the freedom for self-expression is extremely limited or even absent, particularly when it comes to expressing emotions. Furthermore, some subjects require students to memorize facts and rules and repeat or apply these in order to achieve good marks and demonstrate the requisite knowledge of which that subject consists. In such subjects there is no room for creative, distinctive self-expression or even an emotional response to the subject matter.

If learning how to appropriately, creatively or uniquely express one's own feelings and thoughts is deemed valuable, the arts seem to be an excellent place to endeavour to do so. The arts are conducive to such self-expression, particularly given emotions are often difficult to accurately portray and art media offer various abstract and creative ways to achieve this. At a time in young children's lives when their linguistic capabilities are under-developed, art as a form of self-expression offers a new artistic vocabulary that is engaging and playful. For teenagers, struggling with self-expression as new feelings arise as they grow and develop, the arts can offer a cathartic medium and the chance to be 'heard' which is often deeply desired at this stage in a young person's life.

This argument assumes that self-expression is a good thing and the arts can assist students with this. All students should be given the opportunity to create artworks in school because they may not have this chance outside of school, either through their families, friends or work or social lives. They may not realize they have a special talent for self-expression using one of the art media available (i.e. music, drama, painting, sculpture, writing, dance, etc.), and even if they are not going to become an artist or even if they are not particularly talented in any art medium, they may find the art medium gives them the chance to express themselves in a way not otherwise afforded to them and this adds a beneficial and positive mode of self-expression to their lives.

However, there are a couple of problems with this argument. The first is the assumption that self-expression is obviously good, valuable, important and, perhaps more significantly, always so. Wrapped up in this idea is the question of whether all forms of expression and all utterances are worthwhile and valuable. This raises the issue of *who* is expressing *what*, and *who* is receiving the work. The contextual aspects of art making, display and reception are significant with respect to the utterances and experiences of artworks. It is not the case that any and all expressions are positive or beneficial – either for those asserting or for those bearing witness to or receiving the expression in question. Even advocates of free speech in a wide, non-restrictive sense do not hold that no speech acts are harmful, it is simply that they maintain the value of such free expression despite any harmful consequences. Alongside the question about the moral value of the content of artistic expressions, there is also the question as to whether or not and how the arts may communicate – directly or indirectly – to its audience (even if that audience comprises only the artist or the students in an art class).

There have been art educators who defend art as a 'fourth "r"', alongside literacy (reading), writing and numeracy (arithmetic), focussing on the importance of students learning arts literacy (Broudy, 1991: 127; York, 1997). There are a couple of ways of making sense of this claim that positions arts education alongside numeracy and literacy. The first interpretation is that the arts benefit the three 'r's' in an instrumental sense, improving results in reading, writing and maths. I will critically engage with instrumental arguments such as these in Chapter 6, but, in short, the empirical evidence of such instrumental benefits is scarce and more research is required in order to establish causal connections such as these and even if such evidence was forthcoming the arts may not be the most direct method of effecting such outcomes (Broudy, 1991: 127; Koopman, 2005: 86). Furthermore, on this understanding of the arts as a form of self-expression, it is not the arts, but, rather, the skills of reading and writing that are doing the expressive work here. This leads us to consider a second interpretation of the arts as a 'fourth "r"'.

The second interpretation is that the arts furnish us with a language – and, hence, mode of expression and communication – of their own. Yet, as Broudy argues (1991: 127), 'attempts to construct arts alphabets are not very convincing. Colors, sounds, textures, gestures, lines, and shapes can be thought of as elements out of which aesthetic images are assembled, but the resulting images cannot be looked up in a standard dictionary for definitions.' If the arts provide us with a form of literacy, it is not that of the traditional sense, and the term 'literacy' cannot be taken too literally (Broudy, 1991: 128). Rather, arts literacy is of the kind which features symbolic and abstract language, replete with metaphors and multiple meanings.

Having said that, Broudy (1991: 128) goes on to acknowledge that there are such skills and techniques of expression that may be learned in arts classes, specifically of the symbolic and subjective kind, and these are notably very good at communicating feeling states. He states:

> That there are skills of expression is witnessed by schools of music, painting, dance, theater, and creative writing. Arts programs in the schools for a very long time have concentrated on developing expressive skills, chiefly in music and the graphic arts. Unfortunately, the skills of expression, i.e., of the making of images that express human import of one sort or another, tend to become less functional for more and more people as linguistic forms are developed. Beyond the age of seven or eight, ordinary language takes the place of imagery as forms of expression for all but a tiny minority of individuals, artists.

This is an astute observation. It is not easier to express ourselves through the arts unless we are extremely proficient with the materials and have the requisite skill set with which to do so. For most of us, it is easier to simply *say* what we mean, rather than attempt to communicate or convey meaning via paint, physical movement or haikus. Broudy (1991: 128) gives the example of learning a second language and how difficult it is to get to the level of proficiency that allows for ease of expression in that second language, particularly when one has recourse to their primary, dominant language. He notes that for the majority of adults the arts may be a pleasant and diverting hobby, but the expression *of* meaning is unlikely to be the main goal or focus of such enjoyment. This is particularly true given that clearly expressing what we wish to convey through art media is difficult and requires technical skills and expertise which, if we lack, may instead prove to be a source of frustration.

Yet this criticism does not deny that art can be, in many ways, far more expressive than linguistic speech. For example, a caricature may convey much about someone's personality without the need for lengthy description. Yet, it is the caricaturist who is adept at expressing a person's personality in this way, not the average person with average drawing ability. So, while Broudy would love to 'think of a citizenry that could express itself in poetry, paint, clay, dance, and drama' (1991: 129), he claims that we grow out of being pleased with our own artistic expressions once we leave 'naïve childhood' behind. Thus, the benefit conveyed of arts education as a form of arts literacy allowing for self-expression is, he argues, not advisable.[3] This is due to the lack of efficiency in using the arts as a form of self-expression and also because it is only the minority of people, namely artists, who truly can and do express themselves through art media. It seems to me that Broudy may be holding up too high a standard for artistic and creative self-expression, as, although I am only a moderately good dancer, by no means very good or expert, I still enjoy the self-expression of movement to music, even without an audience. Yet the pleasure gained in dancing is more than simply that of self-expression. It also includes other aspects such as sociability, exercise, learning a new skill, etc.

Another interesting take on the focus on the arts as a form of self-expression is that this line of argument is often employed with respect to a therapeutic model of art. On this vision, art media are tools to assist individuals in their journey of self-discovery, understanding, representations of trauma and healing. This account paints an instrumental picture of how the arts are useful in relation to psychological aims and methods. This form of self-expression as catharsis may well be constructive, but we must ask whether this is the best defence for arts education in schools? I do not think it best to treat all students as psychologically deficit and in need of healing (through art or by other means). And, if there is a need for catharsis (or psychological support or other forms of stress relief), it is likely that individuals will respond well to various or even quite specific modes of such emotional self-expression. Arguably, there are other equally good or even better ways for students to experience catharsis, such as sport or therapy.

Drawing together a few of the points made thus far, Maxine Greene (2001: 19) notes:

> The arts have been treated either as didactic forms or as decorative devices in education, intended either to improve or to motivate … Art-making and creativity has often been treated therapeutically, sometimes for the sake of pure self-expression or sensory play, both of which are valuable but have little to do

with the arts. They are often located in the affective realm – with the implication that this is an alternative to the cognitive realm.

Even if the arts are a vehicle for self-expression, this is certainly not the only or main reason school children should learn artistic skills and techniques. Self-expression may seem like an obvious educational aim in the contemporary, Western liberal context in which we find ourselves, yet creating art is about so much more than this. As soon as we consider artworks and forms of art and craft making from various times and cultures, we realize they do not always aim at self-expression or distinctive emotional expression. Art is also about belonging, tradition, sharing knowledge and expertise as well as craftsmanship.

Furthermore, as Greene points out above, self-expression for the expressivist is about expressing emotion whereas art can express ideas. Artworks are not always about expressing one's feelings; they may be cognitive and cerebral (i.e. conceptual artworks), they may be about perfection of form and technique (i.e. sculpture and still life paintings), they may be about socio-political and moral critique, all of which is broader than self-expression. Self-expression does not do the arts justice in encapsulating the function or purpose of art and ultimately the expressivist offers an elitist conception of art that excludes or downgrades mass art and craft for their perceived lack of distinctive expression.

In educational terms, if art is only important due to the role it may play in assisting students to express themselves and their distinct emotions, it may be abandoned if a better way to express oneself is discovered. 'Better' may be defined in various ways according to the political, ethical and social mores of the time. It may be decided that it is better to express oneself efficiently, or less creatively, more direct and to the point, in a less atmospheric fashion, seriously ... and so on. All of these are possible options that may be fashionable or useful to a society and could well conflict with the modes of expression the arts are seen to endorse. The expression found in the arts may even be deemed, as Plato worried, antithetical to important pursuits such as the search for truth and wisdom.

Self-expression alone will not do the work required for defending the inclusion of the arts on the curriculum. Yet it may be that even if this isn't the reason we should include the arts on the school curriculum, we may value and applaud the opportunities provided by the arts for students' self-expression. Yet, as Biesta (2017: 117) notes, this self-understanding will not occur if one only seeks to express themselves; it must be supplemented by listening and receiving the perspectives of others, thus allowing for a dialogical or what he terms an existential experience:

> Expressivist approaches to art education run the risk of forgetting that not everything that is expressed, not everything that emerges in the words and deeds of children and young people is necessarily beneficial for their own lives and for the lives they lead with others on a planet with limited capacity to give us everything we desire. … the real educational work is precisely *not* about facilitating expression, but is about bringing children and young people *into dialogue* with the world. It is, after all, there that their expressions can encounter the world, material and social, and that such encounters can provide starting points for figuring out what it might mean to exist in the world in a grown-up way, that is, to exist *as subject*.

Self-expression alone is not the central aim of education, or of arts education. Even if it were, the arts are unlikely to prove the most efficient or easiest way to acquire such an ability. While expressing oneself through various art media is on the whole valuable and honourable, it is also not the case that everything made manifest is good, true, or beautiful and thus worthy of expression for its own sake. Therefore, arguments seeking to defend compulsory arts education on the basis of its merit in terms of assisting students to develop a set of techniques and skills by which they may communicate – directly or indirectly – their unique and distinctive thoughts, feelings and emotions fail. Such creative expression is important, particularly for children and young people, but on its own, this is not the best justification for teaching the arts in schools.

Art as moral formation

Another argument for including the arts on the curriculum is due to the benefits the arts confer in terms of students' moral development. Some of the very first books written for children were intentionally morally instructive, and philosophers such as Mary Wollstonecraft (1792) highlighted the important role of stories in teaching children moral rules and appropriate etiquette. Contemporary arguments in favour of the arts developing young people's moral dispositions often align with the virtue ethics tradition that sees the cultivation of moral habits as not just a good thing to do but vital for leading a good and pleasant (flourishing – *eudaimonia*) life. This argument will often refer to the power of music and narrative artworks in particular (especially poetry and literature) to support the habituation of relevant moral emotions such as sympathy, empathy and compassion, which assist the moral agent to treat others with care, respect and attentive concern for their well-being.

Briefly, virtue ethics dates back to Ancient Greece and the writings of Aristotle (385–323 BC). Aristotle sought to understand moral decision making as grounded in real-life experience, guided by the idea that we practise certain habits until they become ingrained character traits: virtues or vices. The idea here is that the virtues are good character traits that are guided by rationality and practical habits, helping one to lead a happy (the Greek word *eudaimonia* best translates as 'flourishing') life. Virtues such as honesty, kindness, trustworthiness and courage are all pro-social habits that help us to get along with others and thus enable us to be moral, social beings. The individual virtues are said to lie in the middle of two extremes – the golden mean between two vices. For instance, courage is the virtue that lies between cowardice, on one side, and rashness, on the other. Instead of considering what action is the correct one, the virtue ethicist asks, 'What would the virtuous person do?' It is said that the virtuous person would behave in the right way at the right time for the right reasons. If someone was drowning, the virtuous person would help in a way that was commensurate with their abilities and appropriate to the context in which they found themselves, and, importantly, they would want to help; they would be moved by appropriate emotions to act in accordance with this virtuous character trait.

David Carr defends the inclusion of the arts and literature, particularly poetry due to its affective quality (2005: 149), on the curriculum in order to help students make sense of and cultivate their own appropriate cognitive and emotive responses which, in turn, may improve their character. His argument concludes:

> The power of art and literature to deepen and extend our understanding of ourselves; the world and our relations with others seems clear enough, and may be taken to vindicate the insight ... that such studies have a key role to play in the wider moral (as well as aesthetic) formation of human virtue, character and sensibility.
>
> (Carr, 2005: 149)

And yet Carr is aware of the subtlety involved in defending this claim. He notes (Carr, 2017) that there is bound to be conflict between various conceptions of virtues and that identifying manifestations of virtues may only be usefully understood contextually. However, the seeming lack of moral normativity here is akin to the moral decision-making capacities of human beings. What we witness in stories as well as in 'real life' moral dilemmas is the *narrative*-like structure adopted when trying to think through and work out what is the right thing to do. We tell stories about the dilemmas we face when we ask others for advice, and they imaginatively enter the scenario we have sketched in order to think and feel *their* way through to see what they might do in this situation. Carr writes:

> The basic logical form of moral understanding is *narratival* and well exhibited in the wealth of stories of human travail and endeavor of human cultural and literary inheritance.
>
> (Carr, 2017: 1–2)

It is for this reason that narratives are a brilliant source of insight into such complexity of moral understanding, feeling and the virtues.

Happily, Carr does not succumb to the despair of cultural moral relativism, whereby the tension between the virtues and their manifestation in different places at different times is, as Alasdair MacIntyre (2007) laments, conceptually incommensurable. There is a real worry that my version of courage (a virtue) is equivalent to your version of cowardice (a vice), or another person's version of rashness (also a vice). Yet, despite contextual variances, we must recognize the normative aspect of shared human values and virtues that are common to all and resist the collapse into relativism (MacIntyre, 2007; D'Olimpio, 2018: 13). Otherwise, if morality was subjective, then moral learning would simply be about etiquette and moral knowledge as such would not exist. Yet, Carr claims, we need not be so disheartened:

> On the contrary, there is clearly much for children and young people to learn – precisely to come to know and understand – about the value and implications of justice, honesty, courage, self – control, integrity, and other qualities of moral character for a flourishing human life. Moreover, as philosophers from Aristotle to Alasdair MacIntyre have clearly shown – and as this paper has sought to endorse – this is an enterprise that may be greatly assisted by the (judicious) teaching of good literature.
>
> (Carr, 2017: 15)

As he notes, Carr follows in a fine tradition of philosophers such as Martha Nussbaum, Iris Murdoch and Henry James in defending novels as a source of moral knowledge.

On accounts such as these, moral truth is understood as wider than that of a solely propositional account. The practical knowledge of *phronesis* – wisdom – situates knowing *how* and knowing *what it is like* alongside knowing *that* in terms of importance. For instance, I may know that it is good to be kind, but knowing how to actually perform kind actions is a more nuanced form of moral knowledge. And it may be that I can learn how to actually *be* kind via moral exemplars – some of which may be friends, parents and teachers, and some of which may be characters in stories. Certain novels, Nussbaum (1990: 162) claims, 'calls forth our "active sense of life", which is our moral faculty'. In this way, readers may develop compassionate responses through caring, imaginative engagement with aesthetically and ethically good works of narrative art. As Susan Sontag (2007: 12) notes,

> a deep, lifelong engagement with the aesthetic cannot, I venture to say, be duplicated by any other kind of seriousness. Indeed, the various definitions of beauty come at least as close to a plausible characterization of virtue, and of a fuller humanity, as the attempts to define goodness as such.

Nussbaum argues that if we engage in a sympathetic manner with the characters and scenarios depicted within narrative artworks, we may practise a 'loving attitude' or caring disposition that is useful in application to the real world. By practising this moral attitude in relation to characters in stories, we are protected in a safe fictional space which makes it easier to try to imaginatively engage with other perspectives as well as to reflect on our own character traits:

> The 'potential space' of aesthetic activity is a space with which we investigate and try out some of life's possibilities. … the reader or spectator of a literary work is reading or watching the work, but at the same time reading the world, and reading her own self.
>
> (Nussbaum, 2001: 243)

Similarly, Iris Murdoch claims that, in art,

> we are presented with a truthful image of the human condition in a form which can be steadily contemplated, and indeed this is the only context in which many of us are capable of contemplating it at all. Art transcends selfish and obsessive limitations of personality and can enlarge the sensibility of its consumer.
>
> (Murdoch, 1970: 84)

Practising such loving responses may eventually result in this moral disposition (in which compassion is defined as a rational emotion and a virtue) becoming habituated and, over time, engrained in our character. Yet Nussbaum points out that her argument does not apply to *all* works of art, or all narrative artworks:

> One can think of works of art which can be contemplated reasonably well without asking any urgent questions about how one should live. Abstract formalist paintings are sometimes of this character, and some intricate but non-programmatic works of music (though by no means all). But it seems highly unlikely that a responsive reading of any complex literary work is utterly

detached from concerns about time and death, about pain and the transcendence of pain, and so on – all the material of 'how one should live' questions as I have conceived it.

(Nussbaum, 1998a: 358)

The kind of effect stories can have is difficult to quantify or articulate in any more than a correlative manner, particularly the moral impact of narratives. Any causal impact of stories must be subjective and contextual, yet it seems reasonable that the engaging nature of storytelling is something that appeals to human psychology. Stories and images can activate emotions and stimulate ideas which can, in turn, motivate action. Furthermore, narrative artwork may be understood by people of varying education and age levels and, in this way, is much more inclusive than, say, a technical work of moral philosophy. On this argument, we can defend stories as central to moral education, and also make a case for why teachers are required to assist their students to learn how to engage with such stories in a particular way. Yet there are some limitations to this argument, even if one is sympathetic to it.

Firstly, Nussbaum, Murdoch and James are referring to a small number of *aesthetically and ethically good* narrative artworks, which invite questions about *which* artworks should be used in educational settings, how we judge them, both aesthetically and ethically, and how we should use them, pedagogically, in educational settings. (I have written about this elsewhere (D'Olimpio, 2018; D'Olimpio and Peterson, 2018), so I will set aside this debate for now.) Secondly, this kind of argument doesn't refer to writing stories, or engaging with the many other artforms and varied media. It refers to *reading* as a potentially moral act. Which is lovely, but that only defends the inclusion of books and stories on the curriculum, not of art more generally, and the necessity to *read* itself already justifies this claim. While there are others who refer to the morally educative potential of music and poetry, there is a similar problem. Again, these arguments refer to using certain artworks in specific ways rather than focussing on why creating and appreciating artworks *per se* is an important thing to do and thus the argument doesn't defend aesthetic education *per se*.

Assuming we are able to defend the creation and reception of the arts as a tool for moral improvement, should this justify the inclusion of art and aesthetic education on the curriculum? This idea is not a new one given that art has historically been used as a mode of moral formation and communication, particularly imparting religious ideas, mores and lessons to the general public.

Up until the eighteenth century and the Enlightenment, paintings were full of religious symbolism that 'read' as illustrated virtuous texts. Yet history also reminds us that certain texts, symbols and ideas were deemed virtuous and praised, commissioned and displayed, while others were censored and destroyed. Such decisions were made by those in positions of power and authority. So the question of *which* artworks and *which* or *whose* values is inescapable here, and this inevitably highlights the concern to do with whose voices are neglected or omitted.

In fact, I have a lot of sympathy for the idea of using artworks to cultivate compassionate responses in young people. I *do* think there are ways to find good (aesthetically and ethically), inclusive artworks and use them in interesting and creative ways in educational spaces. So I am not against the argument that we can and do use art in morally formative ways. Nevertheless, I do not want to defend the inclusion of the arts on the curriculum using this argument. My concern is that, in this argument, the arts are being offered up as a tool for moral formation, rather than being valued for their own sake for the aesthetic experience they afford.

We have seen that the defences mounted in favour of the role that the arts may play in cultivating good moral character have referred to a small handful of aesthetically and ethically *good* narrative artworks, such as poetry and literature that form the Western canon (going by the examples Nussbaum, Carr and others use). Even if we support this argument, it only offers a defence of careful, close reading of certain narrative artworks. Even if we extend this argument to include other artworks, it does not immediately apply to arts making. So, while I fully endorse the claims that engaging with narrative artworks should be encouraged and may promote virtuous dispositions, particularly when supported by engaging, child-centred pedagogies, this argument is insufficient for my purposes here. Defending the inclusion of reading *some* artworks on the curriculum does not defend the multiple arts and arts making alongside critical reception.

Furthermore, defending the arts on the curriculum due to their capacity for moral education is a tricky argument to defend in causal terms – the best one likely to manage is a strong correlative argument. Despite the fact that we may defend the role for schools to play in moral formation, it may not be that the arts are the best way to cultivate moral habits in children, and the use of narrative artworks for this purpose may even diminish the value of the aesthetic experience in favour of that of the moral value of the work (I return to the complex and intriguing issue of aesthetics and ethics in Chapter 7). But, even if this is not the case and the use of stories is perfectly suited to teaching ethics in classrooms, it reduces aesthetic education to moral education, and thus will not do as a defence of aesthetic education.

Conclusion

In this chapter I have critiqued two arguments that seek to defend arts education on the basis of, firstly, the role art has to play in supporting self-expression, and, secondly, a defence of the arts in relation to their role in supporting moral improvement. There is a central problem that the two arguments share that render them unsuitable for justifying compulsory aesthetic education in schools. The arguments that rely on the arts as a form of moral improvement or self-expression focus on educational aims that are peripheral to the central concerns and purpose of art. Yes, it is the case that some artworks will help to improve people's moral sensitivity (but these may not be numerous and examples may not readily be drawn from all art media or styles). It is also the case that some art techniques will equip people with non-linguistic communication tools that provide them with alternate means for self-expression and the exploration of their own emotional states. Insofar as educators want to improve children's moral sensitivity or equip them with non-linguistic communication tools, they would do well to teach these works and techniques. However, such educational interventions do not really qualify as education *in the arts*. What is justified by these arguments is an education through the arts – or using art works and art media to further other lessons (lessons in self-expression and sympathy, for instance).

In contrast to the idea of learning *through* the arts, whereby the arts are employed for *other* purposes – which may be personal, socio-political, ethical, economic, academic or psychological, and also in contrast to the idea of arts-integrated learning, whereby other subject areas may make use of artistic techniques and media in order to support learning in history, mathematics, geography and science – we are not seeking to justify a periodic borrowing of works and techniques from the arts. What we are looking for is a justification of education *in the arts*. For that we need to identify educational aims that require more than a periodic borrowing of artistic tools and an instrumental appreciation of what the arts can do, and instead require immersion in the practices of art making and art appreciation.

In the next chapter I will engage more closely with defences of aesthetic education that seek precisely this kind of essentialist justification, as offered by Elliot Eisner and Maxine Greene. As two significant American theorists who have helped shape and influence arts education policy and practice over the past forty or so years, it is worth considering their well-regarded and influential arguments defending an education in the arts. In both this chapter and the next, it is not that I necessarily deny that the defences offered serve a purpose or hold some value. However, I seek the strongest defence for compulsory arts education and in Chapter 4, I will detail and defend my own position before responding to possible objections to it in Chapter 5.

3

Defending arts education

Introduction

An interesting observation is how it can be extremely difficult to defend the arts – their role in society as well as in our lives and in education – in a way that accounts for the various ways people use and enjoy the arts. It is much easier to try and reduce the value of the arts and thus articulate a role for them which is succinct and reductive. The arts themselves are expansive: it is in their very nature to push boundaries and come up with new and interesting modes of expression (of ideas, emotions, things, etc.) because they are symbiotic with creativity. So, when we seek to defend the various and multiple arts, we tend to offer various and multiple defences – not only of particular artworks or artists or art media, but also for why we believe they should be well regarded (valued), funded (resourced), taught (educated) and practised. Such defences take the form of 'art is important because of x, and y, and z ...' or 'art should be valued for reasons a, and b, and c ...' – resulting in what I call a composite argument.

In the previous chapter we examined two specific arguments in defence of arts education; defences we saw often feature on the arts educational policies of developed Western countries such as Australia, Canada, Aotearoa New Zealand, the UK and the United States. These defences of the arts in relation to education were to do with the role art may play in supporting self-expression, and in supporting moral improvement. The arts may well play a role in supporting students' self-expression and in educating their character or sympathetic emotions. Yet even if this is the case, and there are good reasons to encourage young people to express themselves in constructive, creative ways and to practise feeling sympathy and appropriate moral emotions in order to develop ethical attitudes, I critiqued these defences and argued that these should not be the basis upon which we argue for compulsory aesthetic education across the curriculum. We are seeking a justification of education *in the arts*, an educational defence of arts making, valuing and reception, not a justification for using the arts or artistic techniques for other means and purposes. Before I put forward my defence of the compulsory inclusion of the arts on the curriculum on the basis of aesthetic experience, which plays a vital role in the flourishing life (*eudaimonia*), I will in this chapter take a closer look at two contemporary and influential composite arguments in defence of aesthetic education.

Specifically, I will consider and critique the theories developed by Elliot Eisner and Maxine Greene – two significant American theorists who have helped shape and influence arts education policy and practice in important and positive ways over the past fifty years. Eisner in particular is a key figure associated with discipline-based art education (DBAE) and arts-based research, both of which now dominate approaches to arts education across the West. The work of people like Eisner and Greene has supported the arts and aesthetic education and it is by building upon their work – the work that has gone before – that we continue to seek to robustly and reasonably defend the role art can and does and should play in education, in our lives and in our society. While I will critique these composite arguments, that is not to say that I am unsympathetic to them. On the contrary, there are good, practical reasons to support and agree with these theories, usually in relation to advocating for specific policies and support for arts education, and there are aspects of them I thoroughly endorse. However, I will also demonstrate how Eisner and Greene are guilty of some inconsistencies and why ultimately I do not opt for a composite argument in defence of compulsory aesthetic education.

Historical influences on arts education policies

The legacy of arts education that informs policy and practice in many Western schooling systems, including the UK and Australia, originated in America. Art education could be said to have formally commenced in the mid-nineteenth century in America as a gendered subject with a practical focus. It developed during the twentieth century to focus on craft and the development of young children's creativity (Eisner & Day, 2004/2008) and this history illuminates lasting stereotypes facing arts educators today. Prominent American theorists such as John Dewey (1859–1952), Monroe Beardsley (1915–85), Elliot Eisner (1933–2014) and Maxine Greene (1917–2014) have been hugely influential in shaping arts education. Also emerging from the United States in the 1980s was discipline-based art education (DBAE), formulated by the J. Paul Getty Trust Foundation. This educational programme successfully aimed at bringing the arts into line with existing academic subjects in terms of including requisite testable knowledge, standards and a framework suitable for *all* students, not just those who were artistic or talented. DBAE has been the dominant model of teaching art since the 1990s and involves the art studios, art history, art criticism and aesthetics.

What we noticed in Chapter 1 is that, across Australia, the UK and the United States, the language used in their arts education policies is supportive of the arts by using positive wording with a focus on creativity, innovation and technical skills as educationally valuable. They also make mention of the cultural history tied to place, and there is the highlighting of aesthetic knowledge associated with the arts. The idea of *knowledge* associated with the arts that may be taught, learnt and assessed has been made more explicit through the DBAE approach. The idea of this contemporary approach to arts education often associated with 'cognitivism' – the idea that the arts can convey knowledge – was to ensure that subjects in the arts were supported by a rigorous, academic foundation and the curriculum included conceptual and theoretical content as well as technical skills. DBAE includes art production (art making and technical skills), art history, art criticism and aesthetics (the philosophy of art and art theories). As Wolcott (1990: 101–2) explains:

> This new, broader conception of art education known as discipline based art education, incorporates the four disciplines of art production, art history, art criticism, and aesthetics. By including the four disciplines of art, the art education curriculum will provide students with more content, concepts, techniques, and general information, thus contributing to a greater knowledge of art and the world. Some forms of DBAE will present works of art as central to the curriculum content, allowing students to develop the concepts they learn from the various disciplines. The aim of DBAE is to develop students' abilities to understand and appreciate art; to be able to discuss and evaluate unfamiliar and unusual works of art, including contemporary works of art. As in the contemporary art world, the construction of meaning in works of art is the major issue.

In a later publication, Wolcott goes on to note that such an approach demands more of arts educators and their students in the sense that studying the arts using the DBAE model requires them knowing about art history, aesthetic and art theories as well as relevant socio-historical and cultural contexts. This is in addition to the technical skills of creating artworks in specific media and the competence involved in appraising and analysing artworks. She notes:

> Admittedly this approach entails more work on the part of teacher and student alike. Teachers will have to present works of art in more studied context, knowing

something about the history of art, the artworld, and art theories which will better enable them to explain the artist's intentions, theories of art the work rejects or internalizes, technique, and style. Students will also have to develop a grounding in art theory, art history, and knowledge about the cultural and art historical contexts of the work.

(Wolcott, 1996: 78)

Thus, since the 1990s in the United States and Canada, and since the 2000s in Australia, Aotearoa New Zealand and the UK, we see arts education policies being refined and fleshed out as they become increasingly academic and rigorous. We see this in the development of national curricula that detail aims and objectives, standards and marking rubrics for arts-based subjects that include precisely these 'four disciplines' highlighted by DBAE; namely, art production, art history, art criticism and aesthetics. These alterations reflect similar changes made to the approach to education in general, where more precise aims, objectives and outcomes are detailed for all subject areas and an increasing focus on measurement, evaluation, and evidence of effective delivery and pedagogy is honed to meet such criteria. The justification for educational subjects is often made in terms of outputs which, in turn, emphasizes student progress, measurement and evaluation.

What is clear is that the use of DBAE and language defending the unique form of aesthetic knowledge that is able to be taught, learnt and assessed is a key component of situating the arts as a subject worthy of being taken seriously as an academic subject. This strategy assists in defending its compulsory inclusion in the educational curricula and on school timetables alongside other academic subjects such as mathematics, English and history.

What is interesting about the influence of, in particular, Eisner and Greene upon the policy approaches to arts education and the defences they offer of aesthetic education is that such arguments, like their authors, tie together the practical and the academic; they are equally focussed on practical mastery of skills and techniques and on theoretical knowledge. I shall now examine the theories defended by Eisner and Greene in more detail, starting with the work of Eisner.

Elliot Eisner

Eisner started life as a painter and his doctoral research at the University of Chicago was on children's creativity (Eisner, 2005: 1; Craig, Li & Kelley, 2021). His early writings married creativity, the imagination, education and art, and he argued that teaching was not about getting all children to the same stage at the same time. There was a quick interest in and uptake of his work, and Eisner continued to defend the artistry of teaching, the importance of the arts on the curriculum and the significance of what education could learn from the arts in order to improve schooling.

Eisner identified and differentiated between instructional objectives, problem-solving objectives and expressive outcomes. An instructional objective 'seeks to realize goals whose form and content are already known' (Eisner, 2005: 2). In problem-solving objectives, 'the aim is clear, but the method and form of its solution is not' (2005: 2). Expressive outcomes are attempts to describe the actual outcomes, which may be more or less, or better or worse, than our hopes, aims, intentions or expectations. As Eisner says, 'students learn both more and less than what teachers hope for' (2005: 2), and so expressive outcomes are constructed after the fact, retrospectively reflecting upon what has occurred. This artistic approach to education was applicable beyond the arts, but also very useful specifically to teaching in the arts as it allows for flexibility alongside rigour and a sense of what can and cannot be controlled when it comes to both teaching and learning. As Judson and Egan (2012) appraise:

> [Eisner's] educational images reveal to us that there is no one way to teach. There is no one thing to teach. There is no one tool for assessing student understanding. Through extensive theoretical and practical work, Eisner has shown how our educational practices and the approaches we engage to understand students' educational experiences need to be as diverse as the educational contexts and experiences themselves.

As Eisner's work continued to develop, his focus returned often to epistemological questions about art and subsequently one of the central themes for which his theories are known is his cognitivism about art. He was interested in questions such as 'Does art provide knowledge? Can a work of art be "wrong"? If art provides knowledge, what kind does it provide? Do the arts have anything to teach about the world within which they reside?' (Eisner, 2005: 3).

Eisner defended arts education for its instruction in knowledge because of art's connection to cognition, its ability to help students connect to their individual feelings and imagination, and the various cultural understandings it gave students access to. He passionately declared that 'one of the important contributions that the arts, art educators, and like-minded philosophers have made to American education is the idea that the arts are the products of cognition and that cognition is wider than linguistic forms of thinking. Neither thinking nor knowing should be reduced to words or numbers' (Eisner, 1990: 426). In this way, Eisner defended artistic literacy alongside traditional literacy and numeracy, and he defended the arts as meaningfully contributing to knowledge and understanding, validating its essential role on the curriculum. In his own words, Eisner (1981: 48) argues:

> The arts are cognitive activities, guided by human intelligence, that make unique forms of meaning possible. ... the meanings secured through the arts require what might best be described as forms of artistic literacy, without which artistic meaning is impeded and the ability to use more conventional forms of expression is hampered.

Eisner explains that cognition is the process by which we become aware of our environment and this happens through the use of our senses. Our concepts are the result of us perceiving and interpreting the sensory information we glean from our environment, rather than being linguistic at base (Eisner, 1981: 49). He claims, 'concepts precede their linguistic transformation' (Eisner, 1996, preface, p. ix). We can recall and manipulate the concepts formed from sensory input through the use of our imagination. When expressing what has been understood in this way, to ourselves or others, we require a form of representation and again, we often appeal to one or more of the senses to convey this information and make meaning as a result (Eisner, 1981: 50). Because we all use our senses to represent our understanding of the world, the arts offer a means to express these ideas and concepts through various media. As Eisner (1996, preface: x) puts it:

> The ability to secure meaning in the course of our experience is a basic human need; we all want to lead meaningful lives. But meaning is not simply found; it is constructed. In a sense the ability to 'encode' and 'decode' the meanings constructed from different forms of representation requires a form of literacy. Not literacy in the literal sense, but literacy in the metaphorical sense. Literacy, as I use the term, is the ability to encode or decode meaning in any of the forms of representation used in the culture to convey or express meaning. In this sense, I believe, one of the major aims of education is the development of multiple forms of literacy.

This view conceptualizes 'cognition' as broad, and the creative arts as having a role to play in representing and conveying (specific kinds of) knowledge. This is because how we represent our understanding of a mountain, or the seasons, or a feeling of gratitude will depend on what forms and styles and media we have access to in order to conceptualize and convey that information. As Eisner (1981: 50) explains:

the kind of information that we are able to convey about what we have conceptualized is both constrained and made possible by the forms of representation that we have access to and are able to use. Some of the things an individual knows are better represented by some forms than others. What one can convey about a river that slowly wends its way to the sea will be significantly influenced by the form of representation one chooses to use. The same holds true for portrayals of classrooms, teaching, love affairs, and memorable cities one has visited.

By considering the differences between artistic and scientific forms of inquiry, as well as any similarities, Eisner defended the connection between the arts and arts making and cognition. He usefully argued against a simplistic and reductive dichotomy whereby the sciences were connected to thinking, cognition and the intellect, as opposed to the arts, which were historically associated with emotion. As Nel Noddings (2012) notes, quoting Eisner:

> Eisner was particularly troubled by the artificial and counterproductive separation of the cognitive, affective, and psychomotor dimensions of human activity. He was right to point out that this artificial separation hurts all three dimensions but does special damage to the cognitive: 'Thus there is the irony of cognition becoming increasingly important in educational discourse while it is being robbed of its scope and richness.'
>
> (1979: 83)

If we are able to demonstrate that the arts are connected to cognition, this provides a good rationale for adding the arts to the school curriculum alongside subjects such as the sciences and mathematics, particularly if the aim of education is deemed to be improving our mental abilities and knowledge. Also from this claim, other policy decisions will follow with respect to how art ought to be taught and assessed. This thought is connected to who (or which subject discipline) presents what and how, and how various knowledge forms and media represent things in different ways. Eisner gives the example that dance presents something in a particular way, that is different from painting or sculpture, and we may see the same object or idea differently depending on which representation we engage with. Similarly, mathematics or biology presents an idea to us in a certain way – there are multiple and various ways of seeing that offer us knowledge and understanding.

He says (Eisner, 1981: 51):

> Any form of representation one chooses to use – visual, auditory, or discursive – must also be treated in some way. Some forms tend to call forth one particular

mode of treatment. The treatment of mathematics, for example, is essentially conventional, even though we may recognize its aesthetic qualities. The visual arts, by contrast, tend to emphasize the mimetic and the expressive. Language tends to be treated conventionally and expressively (save for occasional instances of onomatopoeia, which are obviously mimetic). The forms we choose provide potential options. The options we choose give us opportunities to convey what we know and what we are likely to experience.

Thus, on this account, to educate to improve students' cognitive abilities is to educate in the various forms of representation that allow for many diverse ways of representing the world – of making and conveying meaning. To exclude the arts as legitimate forms of representation of concepts and understanding is to do a disservice to students' repertoire of means and modes of communication. The forms of artistic literacy are going to be particularly suited to those who interpret the world and express their ideas and feelings through expressive and mimetic forms.

A strength of the cognitivist approach in relation to the arts is that knowledge on this account is not defined narrowly as only related to propositional forms of knowledge or restricted to an account of knowledge as justified true belief (JTB). On this wider understanding of cognition, knowing *how* and knowing *what it is like* are just as important as knowing *that*.

However, a problem with Eisner's cognitivism is in trying to understand or delineate what exactly art teaches in a unique way, that isn't taught or represented in other subjects. I can understand a representation of a mountain in geography or science as well as in art. This criticism is further complicated by the fact that the arts have so many different ways of representing that object or concept. So, the mountain in question may be painted, or written about poetically, or sculpted, or perhaps expressed through dance and music. Is each representation offering new information about the mountain? And perhaps the most direct, immediate understanding will always be gained from seeing or climbing the mountain. So why do we need the arts for this particular representation to contribute to our knowledge base?

Eisner's cognitivism, which defends the kind of knowledge gleaned from art, accompanies this idea that what counts as knowledge, or perhaps what is deemed to be knowable, may be delineated in various ways in different fields, and this is true both internally in the field or discipline and beyond disciplinary boundaries. This is most obviously true in the case of religious 'knowledge', but may also apply to other fields, including the arts. The fact that this is so is not solely a matter of media: how we use either words or slogans or paint or musical instruments to express and convey ideas; but it is also a matter of politics and social context. Now, these are actually two different issues under discussion here: one is to do with (objective) knowledge, and the other is to with how subjects are taught and what ends up being selected to enter the canon. The first issue asks whether aesthetics offers a unique form or forms of knowledge – from which questions follow such as how do we teach and test this understanding? Eisner's cognitivism sees knowledge, understanding and meaning making as incredibly broad, in an effort to place the importance of the arts and artistic literacy on an equal footing with mathematics and numeracy, and English and traditional literacy. The second issue asks who should get to say what we teach, which examples we use, and what we include on the curriculum as essential or seminal examples of this subject.

In terms of the latter, the politics of what is not taught is just as significant and influential as what is taught. Eisner coined the term 'the null curriculum', commenting that, 'what schools do not teach may be as important as what they do teach' (Eisner, 1979: 83). All subject areas and disciplines contain gaps and blindspots: 'intellectual processes that schools emphasize and neglect [and] content or subject areas that are present and absent in school curricula' (Eisner, 1979: 83, cited in Craig, Li & Kelley, 2021). Eisner was interested in the patterns of dissemination of research, including who would read and cite and teach what and where (Craig, Li & Kelley, 2021). Eisner (2005: 6) explains, 'Forms of representation both reveal and conceal aspects of the world and therefore had not only implications for understanding, but had implications for the politics of the field itself.'

Indeed, Eisner's interest in education is wider than his interest in the arts, but it is his artistic approach that he credits with giving him a way of seeing configurations – such as those of the curriculum – and a keen interest in ensuring schools are creative places that truly educate (Eisner, 2005: 3). His approach is sensible, hopeful and pragmatic. He himself notes that he views idealistic approaches as naïve and wants to make more room for the fact that all decisions and aspirations take place in the real world: a world which has political influences, economical, ideological and other interests that will shape and pull and tug at those making decisions, designing policies, and acting in roles of authority. Therefore, we cannot ignore considerations of politics and power, as such factors effect what may actually be done in certain contexts, and what may be achieved.

A composite argument

While involved in bringing it about that the DBAE approach took prime position in educational approaches to teaching art, Eisner defended the importance of time allocated to the arts on school curricula. Noting that, 'in American schools, the arts receive about two hours of instructional time per week at the elementary level and are generally not a required subject of study at the secondary level' (Eisner, 1992: 592, quoted in Craig, Li & Kelley, 2021), Eisner argued that 'time represents value and opportunity: value, because it indicates what is considered significant; opportunity, because the school can be thought of as a culture of opportunity' (Eisner, 1992: 592). It was the arts, Eisner claimed, that, more than any other subject, put a premium on activities that 'can help students discover the special qualities of experience we call aesthetic' (Eisner, 1992: 595). He commented that 'the arts teach a different lesson. They celebrate imagination, multiple perspectives, and the importance of personal interpretation' (Eisner, 1992: 549). In seeking meaning and aesthetic knowledge through the arts and in conjunction with specific artworks, this approach was encapsulated in DBAE and designed to support 'students to build their capacity to not only appreciate aesthetic ways of knowing but to come to understand the philosophy of beauty through understanding' (Eisner, 1992: 595).

As I mentioned at the start of this chapter, this kind of defence of arts education I call a 'composite argument' because it contains many threads that, jointly and taken together, defend aesthetic education and offer multiple arguments as to why the arts should be compulsory on the curriculum and valued educationally. To explain further why Eisner's defence is composite in this way, we only need to look at the popular poster *Ten Lessons the Arts Teach*, drawn from Eisner's book *The Arts and the Creation of Mind* (2002). The ten lessons are as follows:

1. The arts teach children to make good judgements about qualitative relationships.
2. The arts teach children that problems can have more than one solution.
3. The arts celebrate multiple perspectives.
4. The arts teach children that in complex forms of problem-solving purposes are seldom fixed, but change with circumstance and opportunity.
5. The arts make vivid the fact that neither words in their literal form nor numbers exhaust what we can know.
6. The arts teach students that small differences can have large effects.

7. The arts teach students to think through and within a material.
8. The arts help children learn to say what cannot be said.
9. The arts enable us to have experience we can have from no other source and through such experience to discover the range and variety of what we are capable of feeling.
10. The arts' position in the school curriculum symbolizes to the young what adults believe is important.

The beauty about a multi-pronged argument such as this one is that, even if you disagree with one of the reasons or arguments, there are nine others to back up the same conclusion; namely, that the arts are valuable and ought to be given a position on the curriculum and supported with appropriate resourcing. This is a useful tool if you are trying to effect policy and influence policy makers. The politics of this approach is clever and pragmatic: if you want to effect change you must convince the decision makers in relevant positions of authority of your argument and a multi-pronged argument such as this one can adopt multiple lines of defence, focussed on various stakeholders. Some of the arguments are pragmatic (number 10), others are aspirational (number 8), others still are epistemic claims (number 5), and others are about value or problem-solving skills. Some of these things that the arts purport to teach are more difficult than others to defend, substantiate and evidence. Obviously, in list form on a poster, we are not provided with the justifications for these claims, they are offered to us as an appeal to authority.

While there are some very convincing claims made in this list of ten (especially numbers 2 and 3), most of them have exceptions and caveats associated with them, thereby making them difficult to defend universally. For instance, while the arts may indeed demonstrate to students that small differences can have large effects, this is not unique to the arts, and is also not always true. Any scientific experiment will also demonstrate that something small may produce a bigger effect and we can learn through the use of telescopes and microscopes that sometimes small differences are deceptively significant or large in impact. But sometimes something small actually is insignificant! And other claims on the list are vague (especially numbers 7 and 8). In some respect we are always 'thinking through a material' – depending on what is meant by 'material' (does our corporeal body count?) and what is meant by 'thinking' (is Eisner referring to forms of expression of thinking rather than instinctual reflexes?). There is a similarly woolly term used when it is claimed the arts help children to 'say what cannot be said': what is meant by 'say' here, given that if it truly cannot be said then how could we say it? While some of the claims seem unique to the arts (or are phrased in this way), others are not – for instance, number 10: it is true that the position of any subject on the curriculum tells children and parents something about how that subject is (or is not) valued. So, taken together, these ten arguments are probably stronger than the sum of their parts: at least in a political manner in terms of their impact; but this does not mean this list of arguments defending arts education is the best or strongest defence available.

As a fan of lists of 'ten things', Eisner and Barone have also created a list of ten ideas that underpin arts-based research. This list also acts as a defence of arts-based research along with explaining the approach in a succinct manner. Again, each of these items is explained in more detail in their book, *Arts Based Research*, but here are Barone and Eisner's (2011: 164–71) ten 'fundamental ideas' of arts-based research:

1. Humans have invented a variety of forms of representation to describe and understand the world in as many ways as it can be represented.
2. Each form of representation imposes its own constraints and provides its own affordances.
3. The purpose of arts-based research is to raise significant questions and engender conversations rather to proffer final meanings.
4. Arts-based research can capture meanings that measurement cannot.
5. As the methodology for the conduct of research in the social sciences expands, a greater array of aptitudes will encounter forms that are most suited to them.
6. For arts-based research to advance, those who prepare researchers will need to diversify the development of skills among those who are being taught.
7. Arts-based research is not only for arts educators or professional artists.
8. In arts-based research, generalizing from an n of 1 is an acceptable practice.
9. The aim of arts-based research is not to replace traditional research methods; it is to diversify the pantry of methods that researchers can use to address the problems they care about.
10. Utilizing the expressive properties of a medium is one of the primary ways in which arts-based research contributes to human understanding.

This list shares some similarities with the list of ten things that the arts teach, in that arts-based research is also offering to teach us things that other disciplines do not, and an arts-based approach to knowledge and understanding (and research) has traditionally been maligned and criticized as unscientific or woolly, too sentimental and subjective, inconsistent and capricious. Some similar criticisms may be aimed at the arts and, by extension, arts education (especially in relation to assessment, objectives and questions about standards). While defending what the arts can teach us, and defending arts-based research, Eisner on the one hand sought to ensure arts education was more rigorous, consistent and accepted amongst other more academic subjects and scientific approaches, and, at the same time, strove to defend what was unique and significantly of value about the arts.

There is a pragmatic reason why I think this was a good approach to take and at the time in which Eisner adopted this approach, it gained traction and influenced educational policy. His defences of the arts, and of arts-based research, have helped to lend support to arts-based subjects and associated disciplinary approaches, including to research. It has also resulted in the now widely used DBAE approach, which I endorse because it combines aesthetic education (theory and criticism) with the practical skills associated with arts making. Theoretically, a composite argument works in a unique way. By tying together threads of various defences and arguments, the resulting knot of a multi-stranded rope is stronger than any one of those threads alone. And due to their multiple nature, the arts do indeed serve many functions, so this defence of the arts can well be considered appropriate. However, it is also the case that when pulled apart, the rope can become frayed and if a couple of the strands of argument are discredited, or removed from the rope, to that extent the resulting threadbare rope is weakened. And, as I have just demonstrated, quite a few of the ten justifications can be unravelled.

While clearly defending what we can learn from the arts and illuminating what is uniquely valuable about arts-based approaches, Eisner went even further than this and argued that other academic disciplines and subjects could learn a lot from the arts. So instead of moulding the arts on academic disciplines and changing what were some strengths of arts-based approaches, Eisner also claimed that academic disciplines could be more artistic and, in this way, more like the arts. He writes:

> The most recent evolution of my thinking pertains to the question, "What can education learn from the arts about the practice of education?" With this question, I try to turn the tables. The current educational policy push in the United States is highly mechanistic and based on the assumption that subject fields such as the arts are mushy and that their improvement requires becoming

"rigorous," a widely used term for both evaluation and educational research. The position that I have taken is that the arts need not come to look like the way some people believe academic fields should function, but rather academic fields would do quite well to try to look more like the arts when the arts are well taught. Put another way, I am trying to develop the view that artistry could serve as a regulative ideal for the ways in which we think about the means and ends of education. The arts should not look more like the academic fields; academic fields in practice and conception would do well to look more like the arts.

(Eisner, 2005: 6)

Put bluntly, while such sentiments are positive and garner much support from those who practise and endorse the arts and arts-based researchers, they are also rather vague and ephemeral. It is tricky to pin down what this means and what it might actually look like in practice. To his credit, Eisner worked at explaining, exploring and fleshing out such arguments for many years over the course of his academic career, and this is an ongoing project to which others – theorists, practitioners, educators, administrators and art-lovers – will continue to contribute, evolving and carrying forward this legacy. However, it is inevitable that such people will disagree and clash with their ideas of what the original sentiment means. This may not be a problem if there is room for 'the more the merrier', but if there is argument over the 'best' way to do things (which surely there will be, and in light of the political and economic context in which we all work there must be), then this project becomes more difficult or fractious.

A unified vision is not necessary, but if there is a strong, rational argument for the necessity of aesthetic education, this could be a good thing, especially as it aims for the truth: why are the arts so important and significant in our lives, such that we believe every child should learn them? I think the arts do many things: including many of the things Eisner lists. However, the real reason I believe we should necessitate their lessons is because of the role they play in producing and supporting access to aesthetic experiences, which, in turn, occupy a vital role in the flourishing life. Therefore, in the next chapter, I will devote my attention to this one focussed argument, given I have pointed out the weaknesses in Eisner's composite argument. But not before I consider the composite argument defended by Greene.

Maxine Greene

Maxine Greene spent most of her academic career at Columbia University's Teachers College, of which she was the first female member of faculty in the philosophy of education department when she joined in 1965. Following in the steps of her academic predecessor, John Dewey, she contributed to public life in significant ways such as by occupying the role of Philosopher-in-Residence at the Lincoln Center Institute for the Arts in Education from 1976 to 2012 (The Maxine Greene Institute, 2022). In her work with this educational arm of the performing arts centre, Greene inspired the creation of an arts-focussed high school, which is now called the Maxine Greene High School for Imaginative Inquiry. Their mission statement, available from the school website, reads as follows:

> At The Maxine Greene High School for Imaginative Inquiry we work to infuse our interdisciplinary curriculum with experience in, and reflective study of, the arts in accordance with the model created by the Lincoln Center Institute for the Arts in Education. We believe that encounters of this sort release imagination and open unexpected intellectual possibilities that provoke students to reach beyond themselves as they "look at things as if they could be otherwise" and, most significantly, encourage civic dialogue which empowers all of the members of our diverse school community to work towards a more just, humane and vibrant world.

In Greene's obituary published in the *New York Times* (Weber, 2014), it is noted that she 'extolled the virtues of the Thoreauvian concept she called "wide-awakeness"', to which the multiple arts were particularly well suited. Unlike Thoreau, Greene believed such aesthetic stirring could be democratized and ultimately, 'Dr. Greene believed that creative thinking and robust imagining were the keys not just to an individual's lifelong learning but to the flourishing of a democratic society.'

Greene is best known for her defence of aesthetic education, which takes the form of what I am calling a composite argument. It is noted that her philosophical writing style is 'literary' (Lake, 2010) and even on the website for the Maxine Greene Institute it is noted that 'aesthetic education' is defined in a number of ways. This inconsistency leaves us without an appropriate definition of aesthetic education and some definitions expressed in her writings appear woolly, using words that are tricky to pin down because they can mean more than one thing. Yet Greene's definition of aesthetic education is worth examining not only because of its influence, but also because of its connection to aesthetic experience.

In her seminal book, *Variations on a Blue Guitar: The Lincoln Center Institute Lectures on Aesthetic Education* (2001: 5–6), Greene writes:

> 'Aesthetic', of course, is an adjective used to describe or single out the mode of experience brought into being by encounters with works of art. 'Education',

as I view it, is a process of enabling persons to become different, to enter the multiple provinces of meaning that create perspectives on the works. To enter those provinces (be they those identified with the arts, the social sciences, the natural sciences), the learner must break with a taken-for-granted, what some call the 'natural attitude', and look through the lenses of various ways of knowing, seeing and feeling in a conscious endeavour to impose different orders upon experience.

...

'Aesthetic Education', then, is an intentional undertaking designed to nurture appreciative, reflective, cultural, participatory engagements with the arts by enabling learners to notice what is there to be noticed, and to lend various works of art their lives in such a way that they can achieve them as variously meaningful. When this happens, new connections are made in experience: new patterns are formed, new vistas are opened. Persons *see* differently.

The connection of aesthetic education to experience is obvious, and again, very Deweyan in the manner of learning by doing. However, there is also a slippage between what aesthetic education is and what the effects of it may be. In her 'Notes on Aesthetic Education', which is sub-titled 'An initiation into new ways of seeing, hearing, feeling, and moving ...' Greene commences with 'we are interested in education here, not in schooling.' ... 'education signifies an initiation into new ways of seeing, hearing, feeling, moving. It signifies the nurture of a special kind of reflectiveness and expressiveness, a reaching out for meaning, a learning to learn' (2001: 7). Elsewhere, she writes, 'The arts, in particular, can release our imaginations to open up new perspectives, identify alternatives. The vistas that might open, the connections that might be made, are experiential phenomena; our encounters with the world become newly informed' (Greene, 1995: 18).

Greene does not offer an analytical definition of art. She, instead, treats the concept more fluidly, seeing artworks as discursive objects with which one may engage in a hermeneutic fashion. For example, when engaging with Weitz's theory, she comments on how it is more important to talk about what aesthetic theory can do than try and settle a definition of art:

Morris Weitz, speaking from quite another philosophic vantage point, seems to me to be saying something relevant in this regard when he remarks that, even though theories of art fail when it comes to defining art, aesthetic theory cannot be called worthless:

Indeed, it becomes as central as anything in aesthetics, in our understanding of art, for it teaches us what to look for and how to look at it in art. What is central and must be articulated in all the theories are their debates over the reasons for excellence in art – debates over emotional depth, natural beauty, exactitude, freshness of treatment, and so on, as criteria of evaluation – the whole of which converges on the perennial problem of what makes a work of art good. To understand the role of aesthetic theory is not to conceive it as definition, logically doomed to failure, but to read it as summaries of seriously made recommendations to attend in certain ways to certain features of art. [Weitz, The Role of Theory in Aesthetics, 1959: 155]

I appreciate the insistence that 'art' be treated as an open concept; and, although I do not share Weitz's commitment to conceptual analysis, I respond to his emphasis on the 'expansive, adventurous character of art' (p. 152). Because I would relate his various proposals to processes of self-understanding on the part of individuals actually experiencing art, I see his stress on the need to attend as leading into an ongoing hermeneutic (a term he would never use).

(Greene, 1977: 288)

Greene was, like Eisner, keen to defend the statutory status of the arts on the curriculum. She claimed that aesthetic education is not an optional extra, but, rather, 'integral to the development of persons – to their cognitive, perceptual, emotional, and imaginative development' (Greene, 2001: 7). In these claims, we see Greene here invoking the ideal of education for the whole child. This holistic approach does not prioritize the rational mind at the expense of the emotions, and it does not operate in a dichotomy of thinking versus feeling. A whole child approach to education, following Dewey, must include thinking, feeling and doing. And it is the experiential aspect of the arts that Greene believed could offer unique and irreplaceable forms of understanding. The way arts educators could seek to develop 'a more active sensibility and awareness in our students' (2001: 8) was via initiating them into aesthetic experiences, which involved engagement with the arts that resulted in feeling-responses and associated meaning making.

For Greene, the meaning that may be made from engaging with the arts – both creating and appreciating artworks – has connections to the wide sense of knowledge defended by Eisner. Cognition is not absent in aesthetic experiences and, Greene argues, there is an experience to be had that connects the artwork to cognitive understanding via a capacity to see, to hear and to attend (2001: 9). Even receiving an artwork is not a passive process as 'perception is an active mode of paying attention to – of reaching out to, of going towards the work, of being open to it' (Greene, 2001: 13). Greene notes that aesthetic experiences are experienced and understood against the background of our own personal lived experiences, and that arts educators themselves need to possess a heightened sensibility and appreciation for the arts if they hope to bring it about in others.

There is much to like about the composite arguments detailed in a lyrical fashion by Greene, yet ultimately this account must be rejected as inconsistent and ultimately it will not do the work we need it to do to justify the mandatory inclusion of the arts on the curriculum. While Greene places aesthetic experience in a central role for defending the value of arts education, she specifically ties aesthetic experience to artworks, thereby offering a circular definition of aesthetic experience as the experience gained from engaging with artworks. She writes, '"Aesthetic", of course, is an adjective used to describe or single out the mode of experience brought into being by encounters with works of art' (2001: 5). Elsewhere she writes, 'Aesthetic experiences ... involve us as existing beings in pursuit of meanings. They involve us as historical beings born into social reality. They must, therefore, be *lived* within the contexts of our own self-understanding, within the contexts of what we have constituted as our world' (Greene, 1977: 293).

Thus, for Greene, the term aesthetic experience refers to the particular experience evoked by engaging in a particular way with artworks. Yet, as we see in Dewey (1934), aesthetic experiences may be induced by nature as well as by art, and, in fact, Greene acknowledges this even while elevating the role of art objects in affording such experiences. She writes (2001: 53):

> Aesthetic experience, and aesthetic education, presumes that there are certain objects and events that give rise to specific kinds of experiences. The natural world may do this, but artworks are deliberately made for the sake of such experience. This is why they are sometimes called privileged objects. But if they are to come into existence for you as an aesthetic object, they need to be attended to in a particular way. They do not automatically reveal this experience to the viewer.

Greene's tripartite definition of aesthetic experience includes a focus on the object with which we are engaged, plus the experience resulting from such engagement, and, significantly, the way in which we attend to the (art) object in order to affect such (aesthetic) experiences. She notes, 'Aesthetics ... has to do with our reflections upon our encounters with works of art' (2001: 57). And it is this attentiveness or mode of perception she highlights as an educational imperative – this is what we can teach and learn, and it is what the arts themselves can teach and learn – a way of seeing. Greene claims (2001: 45):

There is a particular liveliness and energy with which the mind is activated when works of art are attended to so that the qualitative details emerge and come together, until there is a perception of a whole. That liveliness and energy are in part due to the fact that, in an authentic aesthetic encounter, we are able to recognize how much depends upon our presentness, our attentiveness, our willingness to go out to the work at hand.

The art teacher and the arts classroom play an important role here, with Greene pointing to how they create an almost 'magical' space which has room for students to make use of their imagination by breaking free from the routine, the useful and the conventional in order to enter into another, aesthetic space. It is never exactly clear how we differentiate between these spaces – the normal (the mundane? The routine?) versus the aesthetic – except that Greene offers adjectives illustrative of heightened sensory experiences to describe the latter.

While this sounds positive, there is much slippage in Greene's work and her focus shifts, as sometimes she emphasizes perception and sensibility, and other times she privileges meaning making, and in still other places the emphasis is on feeling. Her theory is also ultimately quite demanding on arts teachers. She clearly states that in order to affect such shifts in perception and encourage such creative, imaginative ways of seeing, arts teachers themselves must have this broader or more attuned sense of perception. She challenges (2001: 46):

> Teachers will only be in a position to make such experiences available to your students if you take the time to cultivate your own informed awareness, if you allow *your* own minds to be activated, *your* feelings to be aroused, *your* imaginations to be released for the sake of bring these works into being for yourselves.

We can see here that the written word is speaking directly to teachers at this point. The 'your' is emphasized in relation to the arts teacher. But elsewhere, Greene appears to be making a wider point, addressing a more generalized audience, and not solely those (such as arts teachers) who are already convinced of the value of aesthetic education.

Thus, as we have started to see, in many places in her work, Greene claims the significance of aesthetic education is that it enables *individual* and *personal* change through the modes of perception and experience and meaning making it offers. And this may take place through the art object, and through the mode of attention we pay to the object in question. But elsewhere she also argues that aesthetic education affords *social* change by means of its offering new lens on ideas, experiences and concepts and by presenting new perspectives than those we have already considered. In this way Greene is defending a composite argument. There are multiple reasons Greene gives that, taken together, highlight the importance of teaching students the arts and aesthetics. However, it is not solely the arts that may achieve these benefits, even if the arts are uniquely qualified for these aims. And it is not clear exactly how the art objects and their associated aesthetic experiences are extra-ordinary. While Greene acknowledges the link between the aesthetic (objects, mode of perception and experiences) and the everyday (à la Dewey), it is unclear where one stops and the other begins, or how we determine when we have stepped from the ordinary into the extraordinary:

> To teach persons to attend, however, to remain within the form, to uncouple physically from the everyday, is not to tell them that the emotions they experience, the visions they see, must be purely aesthetic. We do not want to communicate the formalist creed that aesthetic experiences have nothing to do with other kinds of feelings, with life histories, with the world.
>
> (Greene, 2001: 40)

While this connectedness to the world is a positive aspect to Greene's theory, it is unclear how she might distinguish an art object from a natural object or from something that is not-art. She prioritizes the aesthetic experience, but this is defined in terms of the art object, despite it being clear that aesthetic experiences may be gleaned elsewhere and she hasn't defined art in the first instance. Using superlative adjectives, Greene commends the role for aesthetic education, and yet there are so many reasons given as to how and why aesthetic education matters. It is difficult to keep track of her account for the role of the arts in education, and in life. While it is the case that these composite arguments contain important, attractive and significant threads that may serve strategic purposes, they are also often woolly and inconsistent. There is a role for composite arguments in defending aesthetic education but I would say that this role most likely depends on who it is they are aimed at and what they are trying to convince those people of – be they policymakers or teachers themselves.

Conclusion

In this chapter I have engaged critically with the composite theories defending aesthetic education developed by Elliot Eisner and Maxine Greene. Eisner and Greene have been influential in shaping arts education policy and practice, and we see evidence of Eisner's theory in particular in the discipline-based art education (DBAE) approach to arts education. DBAE remains dominant in developed Western countries – some of whose specific arts policies we examined in Chapter 1. Eisner and Greene both enlisted a philosophical as well as a practical approach to their work. While keen to accurately define key terms and concepts such as aesthetic education, aesthetic experience and aesthetic knowledge, they were also invested in the arts being well taught and enjoying an established place on the curriculum.

Philip Taylor (1996) in his introduction to his edited book, *Researching Drama and Arts Education*, makes reference to Maxine Greene's essay 'The artistic-aesthetic and curriculum' in which Greene warned of political forces that would shape the school curriculum in the arts, seeing the arts take on a political agenda rather than an educative one. This concern reflects the worry Eisner also voiced and includes the misuse of seeking cognitive outcomes from the arts. Greene, like Eisner, wanted to avoid the assessment of the arts (and thus the objectives of arts or aesthetic education) from being reduced to narrow, measurable goals such as those framed by reductive scientific or empirical paradigms (note that this is not to say that all scientific and empirical paradigms are reductive) or those shaped by political interests. Rather, Greene waxes lyrically, 'The test, finally, is in the aesthetic experiences we can make possible, the privileged moments through which we can enable our students to *live*' (1977: 294, my italics). Which is in tension with the current forces shaping education, as Taylor writes, 'the pedagogical climate is constructed by a conventional scientific paradigm which promotes outcomes, controls behaviour, and permits individual reflective turning within foreseen categories and codes' (1996: 3).

One concern being rendered visible here is that ascribing cognitive outcomes to aesthetic education in order to defend its seat at the scholarly table may also work against the arts as subjects that resist the narrow place set at the academic table. Many advocates for the arts express the importance of not reducing the value of the arts to instrumental and measurable gains. However, I agree with Eisner in particular that this is not to deny that there are some measurable cognitive benefits gained from engagement with the arts and an arts-based educational curriculum. If policymakers were to use the arts as a means to promote narrowly cognitive gains such as traditional literacy and numeracy, squashing the expansive notions of artistic literacy and the aesthetic defended by Eisner and Greene, this would be a tragedy and it would flatten the offering of the arts and miss the point of aesthetic education. However, how such gains are measured is another question. I shall return to the topic of instrumental or extrinsic benefits of aesthetic education in Chapter 6.

I have in this chapter sought to present Eisner and Greene's theories and aims charitably. I have done this by contextualizing their theories and their claims, considering not only philosophical critiques of their arguments, definitions and claims, but also by considering practical implications of their work. While there is much to admire and undoubtedly the work of Eisner and Greene helped the arts be taken seriously on the academic curriculum, their composite arguments defending aesthetic education are not defences that I ultimately endorse or wish to employ. Yet I do believe there is value in recognizing that we can learn from the arts, and that cognition plays an important role in aesthetic education.

I will further expand upon my argument in the next chapter as I defend the role for the arts and aesthetic education in helping us to be receptive to and enjoy aesthetic experiences, which contain both affective and cognitive components. While the arts and aesthetic education may indeed do many things, a sound defence of aesthetic education will defend it upon the basis of that to which it is uniquely suited, and which cannot be easily substituted by other subjects or disciplines. For this reason, in Chapter 4, I defend aesthetic education on the grounds of the role played by aesthetic experience in the flourishing life. In this way, my argument will depart from that of Eisner and from that of Greene, even while perhaps one thread of their composite arguments may be found shimmering in the light when we gaze, in turn, at the defence I shall now mount.

4

The centrality of aesthetic experience

Introduction

The arguments defending the inclusion of aesthetic education on the curriculum for reasons of self-expression or due to their role in supporting students' moral development and character formation are inadequate to the task. While each position has something to offer, they are simply not foundational enough for my purposes. Ultimately, defending arts on the curriculum for the sake of self-expression or moral improvement is to defend learning *through* the arts, whereby the arts are employed for *other* purposes. This justifies a periodic borrowing of works and techniques from the arts rather than justifying the role for the arts themselves. What I intend to offer is a justification of education *in the arts*.

Elliot Eisner and Maxine Greene seek to defend aesthetic education and, while I am sympathetic to their arguments, they are what I have called 'composite' due to the multiple, various lines of defence they draw upon to substantiate their case. Because some of the lines of defence they offer are weaker than others, the case taken as a whole is not as strong as it could be, despite the strategic and perhaps political advantage of defending the role for the arts on the curriculum in this way. In addition, as I have detailed in the previous chapter, Greene doesn't offer clearly defined concepts of art, aesthetic experience, or aesthetic education, which I would like to do, while avoiding the charge of circularity when defining aesthetic experience. Furthermore, Eisner focusses quite specifically on the cognitive benefits of arts education, in keeping with educational rhetoric seeking such intellectual and measurable benefits of school subjects, and this is not where the focus of my defence rests. Eisner's definition of what counts as cognitive is extremely broad and it isn't entirely clear on his account what the arts teach that cannot be taught by other subjects. Therefore, I seek a defence of aesthetic education that prioritizes what is uniquely valuable about the arts to secure their place on the curriculum as a mandatory, rather than optional, subject.

The arguments I have critically examined in Chapters 2 and 3 do support the case for defending arts and aesthetic education by offering supplementary justifications for aesthetic education – and they all make valuable and important contributions to articulating and justifying the value of the arts and the multiple roles the arts and aesthetic education play in society. However, my defence focusses on what is uniquely valuable about the arts and why aesthetic education cannot be replaced by any other subject, and why it ought to be compulsory rather than an optional extra. I claim aesthetic education is necessary due to its distinctive ability to offer, invite and invoke aesthetic experience. Such meaningful experiences, of flow, harmony, beauty, the sublime, shock, awe, wonder, etc., are integral to a flourishing life and, therefore, educators have a responsibility to teach students that they may participate in such experiences. It is upon this defence, of the role for aesthetic education in supporting aesthetic experiences and the vital role of such experiences in the flourishing life, that I rest my argument for compulsory school-based aesthetic education.

Life is impoverished to the degree that a person fails to gain *any* aesthetic experience. If one never enjoys some music, or a feeling of artistic movement, or design, the texture of an object, or singing a song, then this is an experience in the flourishing life that is unfortunately and regrettably closed off. Such enjoyment of aesthetic experiences ought to be an option available to those who wish to partake, and this option is made more readily available if one is inducted into it. Of course, people will likely stumble upon a feeling of awe, the sublime, or being moved by the aesthetic features of an object, particularly in nature or when some music suddenly uplifts their spirit. But such aesthetic experiences are more likely to be made present to people in subtle and dynamic ways if they are taught it is an option, particularly afforded by artworks, and if they are educated in an open, receptive attitude that affords them the understanding that art may be experienced in such a manner.

The point of education is to support students to be in the best-possible position to be able to live meaningful, autonomous lives, filled with rich experiences. The arts and aesthetic education are vital to such lives and to such bold, beautiful, moving experiences. Everyone ought to have the opportunity to learn about art, to appreciate and to create art, to critique art and to understand its role in society; historically and theoretically. A life without art is impoverished. In this chapter, I detail the heart of my argument, my defence of compulsory aesthetic education across the curriculum on the basis of the aesthetic experiences the arts afford, and the central role such experiences play in the flourishing life.

I will focus on the distinctive value of artworks, which is their capacity to generate aesthetic experiences. Having said that, as I have already acknowledged over Chapters 2 and 3, the arts may do many things, including supporting self-expression and moral formation through the cultivation of a sympathetic attitude. And it may very well be that it is in these multiple ways that the arts are understood to contribute to the flourishing life. Indeed, as we saw in Chapter 1, on national curricula across the UK, United States, Australia, Aotearoa New Zealand and Canada, education in the arts is valued and often justified in terms of the technical skills associated with arts making, and the cultivation of personal attributes such as self-expression, creativity and imagination, alongside the historical and cultural appreciation afforded by art appreciation and critique. Unfortunately, such positive rhetoric is not accompanied by adequate resourcing and arts subjects are often elective, particularly in senior (high) school, with diminishing student numbers and generalist rather than specialized teachers. As political and societal trends see an increased focus on science, technology, engineering and mathematics (STEM) subjects and associated careers, the arts and humanities are being squeezed and suffer as a result of attempting to defend their value in narrowly utilitarian terms that increasingly correlate to test scores and achievement in other subjects, particularly literacy and numeracy.

While there may be many positive ways in which the arts and art objects may be used in society (i.e. art therapy, artworks as investments, music and drama to improve spatial awareness, or art events as opportunities to gather socially and drink wine and eat cheese), the distinctive value of art objects is that they afford aesthetic experience. And it is upon this foundation that an argument ought to be mounted as to why schooling needs the arts and specialist art teachers, and why all students deserve aesthetic education.

An art instinct

Most people are naturally predisposed to be able to appreciate and enjoy beauty, form, shape, texture, colour, line, movement, sound and other aesthetic features of our environment. By virtue of our capacity for perception and cognition, to experience emotion, receive sensations, and use our imagination, we have an instinct for aesthetic experiences that supports profound feelings, insight and personal meaning making (Schindler et al., 2017). It is these experiences that bring joy, moments of revelation and understanding, feelings of gratitude, awe and shock to our lives, that make our lives distinctly human, and art enriches our lives by being a catalyst and conduit for such experiences and their transcendent effects.

By tapping into a natural instinct or capacity children and young people have, and then encouraging and educating it, aesthetic education affords more opportunities for children to have aesthetic experiences. It does this by teaching them to appreciate art for its form, and value the skills and techniques of the artist, as well as encouraging students to adopt an open, receptive attitude that is conducive to such experiences. These skills, of learning to appreciate art and being open to the beauty and transformative new perspectives offered by artworks, are more likely to be effective when they are taught, practised and encouraged. And while it may be that someone may be overwhelmed by awe and wonder when they stop to observe a sunset, this is simply not always the case or true of everyone, and many artworks are more likely to require a form of education in order for them to be fully appreciated or enjoyed. Art is intentionally and purposefully created to offer its receiver an aesthetic experience; it is this that makes it valuable for its own sake and not for its economic or other value, and why artworks are ideal as the objects with which we should teach students to engage in an open and receptive manner. Furthermore, art is ubiquitous. While nature may be all around us, not all urban schools have ready access to sublime natural landscapes.[1]

There is a connection being made here between natural (human) perception and experience and aesthetic appreciation and experiences. In *The Art Instinct*, Denis Dutton (2009) defends the connection between human beings, art and aesthetic enjoyment as natural and instinctive. He examines historical arguments, theories and practices in support of this claim, commencing with the Ancient Greek philosophers. From the time of Aristotle, we see an argument made for the instinct of human beings, witnessed from childhood, to copy what they see. Aristotle names this 'mimesis' and Dutton (2009: 33) confirms:

> Human beings are born image-makers and image-enjoyers. Evidence for Aristotle can be seen in children's imitative play: everywhere children play in imitation of grown-ups, of each other, of animals, and even of machines. Imitation is a natural component of the enculturation of individuals. That is from the creative side: from the experiential side, human beings enjoy experiencing imitations, whether pictures, carvings, stories or play-acting.

It is our capacity for perceiving the world around us that affords us the ability to appreciate aesthetic qualities and features of our environment. Once we receive the sensations from our senses of sight, touch, hearing, and perhaps even scent and taste, our mind interprets and responds to these stimuli. Our perceptions activate our mental and physiological responses, which include intellectual or cognitive and emotional responses, which interpret what we have seen, heard and/or felt. In this way our mind brings concepts, memories, categories and ideas to bear on what we are experiencing, and our imagination starts to play with these impressions and sensations, from which we derive meaning.

In this way, our aesthetic responses are partly natural and instinctive, but also partly socially influenced via systems of meaning making through which we learn to interpret and respond to the world. As Marcia Eaton (2001: 5) explains:

> Aesthetic response is a basic element of humanity. There are probably biological reasons for this. Some evolutionist theorists believe that aesthetic preferences for certain landscapes (such as savannahs or those with running water) developed from and contributed to survival advantages. Nonetheless, there is also a social determinant to the way in which persons react aesthetically to objects or events.

For instance, these contextual, social influences will include social mores, language, culture, etiquette, assumptions and ideas about gender, sex, class, race, ability, etc. And what is so fascinating is how art can draw upon and then challenge such ideas and concepts and their associated values.

If aesthetic responses are partly learned, then education plays a central role in approaches to art and accounts of aesthetic experience. Like our emotions, Eaton (2001: 12–18) claims that aesthetic responses are learned, culturally bound and socially prescribed and proscribed. While she is careful not to conflate aesthetic responses with emotional responses, Eaton (2001: 18) highlights the important connection between the two:

> I have attempted to show not that aesthetic response is an emotion, but that, nevertheless, things that have been shown to be true of emotions with respect to the ways in which social and cultural features generate and shape them can also be said of aesthetic response. Recognizing this is a crucial first step in understanding the nature of the aesthetic and of aesthetic properties. If those human responses that we describe as 'aesthetic' are not simply inner states caused by a closed set of properties intrinsic to object and events, but rather depend at least in part on the circumstances in which those states and properties are located, then the contextuality of what counts as an aesthetic property must be accounted for in any adequate theory of the aesthetic.

This argument is relevant to educational concerns because it demonstrates that people have a natural capacity to experience the aesthetic features of the world and of art objects, and that they may be educated in ways that refine and support the experience of these to allow for deeper, nuanced and subtle emotional and cognitive responses which in turn afford meaning making and enrich our lives. Furthermore, there is a metacognitive element whereby education (and aesthetic education in particular) will also allow for critical reflection not only on the artwork which prompted a particular response, but also on the response itself.

On this view, the arts may be included in the curriculum as something *everyone* can enjoy and engage in, even if not everyone is likely to consider themselves as an artist or an art connoisseur. And just because we may enjoy aesthetic experiences *naturally* is not to say we should not educate and nurture this capacity such that people can experience it more often and in a more informed way. Most obviously, while it may be fairly easy to enjoy a beautiful waterfall, appreciating or gleaning an aesthetic experience from artworks requires some tutelage.[2] The learning involved may simply be that one needs to be able to read in order to enjoy a story, but when it comes to poetry or Shakespeare, one must also learn *how* to read and understand the narrative or cadence in question. Understanding the structure of a symphony and being able to appreciate its complexity and significance is likely to further enhance the enjoyment and associated emotional experience to be gained from that musical composition (it is difficult to imagine someone understanding, let alone gleaning an aesthetic experience from John Cage's 4'33" – 4 minutes and 33 seconds of silence – without some context). And for some genres, such as opera, for instance, learning about them may then open the door to students being able to gain experiences of passion, awe and shock from an otherwise less accessible artform. I'll never forget being taught Mozart's *Don Giovanni* in high school: my year 11 (fifteen-year-olds) music class learnt about the time period, the structure of the work, about the composer and the story, and then we sat and listened to it, reading along with the score (note that our first language was English and the songs are sung in Italian). There was complete silence and by the end a few of us had tears running down our faces, completely unexpectedly. I might add that our state (not private) school was in a socio-economic area in which many families would be unlikely to play classical or operatic music in their homes.

It ought to be noted that for disabled pupils who may have certain requirements when it comes to their ability to perceive various objects, there needs to be an adaptation or deliberate choices made in order to support their engagement with art objects and performances such that they may perceive them and thereby also glean an aesthetic experience from such engagement. Such perception, engagement and resulting aesthetic experience may not occur without consideration and attention paid to their specific needs and requirements.

Given that there are particular and specific skills and techniques involved in creating art, displaying artworks and receiving artworks in an open yet informed manner, it makes sense that the novice would be well guided by the artist, the art lover or the art critic – the educator – who has experience with and knowledge about artworks, art forms and various media. Active engagement with arts making ensures students have the opportunity to practise creative engagement with media in purposeful and meaningful ways. And, with various media, there are certain techniques that are difficult to mimic or almost impossible to refine on one's own. Technical skills, such as those central to ballet dancing, oil painting, firing ceramics or film editing, need instruction and expertise as well as passion, dedication, commitment and practice. There is a vital role for artists in teaching the arts and teaching the arts can further ensure students have the chance to understand what artworks offer in terms of their value and connection to their lives.

Therefore, there is a natural art instinct: a predisposition to create and enjoy art, and a human capacity for aesthetic experiences. However, this is very much more likely to be included as a regular feature of one's life if it is deliberately cultivated. Making aesthetic experiences more accessible to people involves education. This includes learning about art and how to make, receive and critique artworks. While this claim does not deny that untutored aesthetic experiences may spontaneously occur, and that these may be wonderful, valuable and significant, it is to say that such experiences are more readily available in relation to a much wider scope of objects and stimuli if aesthetic education, particularly in relation to the arts, has taken place. In the next section I will focus more on explaining the nature of aesthetic experience before defending the connection of such experiences to the arts and to the well-lived life.

Aesthetic experience

An aesthetic experience arises from engaging in a particular way – a way that is open and receptive to what is there to be experienced – with *something* – for instance, an art object or art performance or one's surroundings, in nature or a church for example. An aesthetic experience is an extension of *experience*, yet, as John Dewey argues in *Art as Experience* (1934), we must distinguish *an* experience from continuous experience, and aesthetic experience constitutes *an* experience. An experience is both integrated with and demarcated from the rest of experience (Dewey, 1934: 36; Collinson, 1992: 151), and aesthetic experiences may vary widely. The imagination has a central role to play in such experiences and all conscious experience has some imaginative quality for Dewey, through which meaning is gleaned (Collinson, 1992: 153). Significantly, aesthetic experience is connected to the 'something' (an art object, say) and the mode of perception the viewer uses to engage with or contemplate it. As soon as the spectator attends to the art object in question, they invoke mental activity which includes their images, concepts and emotions, all of which are connected to the art object, and it is the aesthetic experience that is emergent, transcendent and valuable.

As I explained in Chapter 2, the experiences that emerge as a result from engaging with artworks are multiple, dynamic and complex. This can make it extremely difficult to define aesthetic experience and when we try to describe the experience associated with a certain object such as a theatre performance or a song or an impressive waterfall, we often find ourselves describing the object. I follow Beardsley (1982: 81) in claiming that an aesthetic experience results when 'the greater part of [one's] mental activity … is united and made pleasurable by being tied to the form and qualities of a sensuously presented or imaginatively intended object' (i.e. an artwork, performance, or natural beauty in the form of a waterfall or sunset) which brings pleasure to the perceiver, but there is more to be said about the nature of aesthetic experiences.

The aesthetic experience can create a moment of focus and stillness as one's attention is absorbed by the object in question and one is expectant as to what will be revealed or felt; in this way the person is open to experiencing what is there to be experienced and receptive to what meaning may be made as a result of the feelings and thoughts that arise in relation to that which provokes this experience. It is this kind of attentiveness that is being referred to when aestheticians say that the artwork is being valued or appreciated for its own sake. Dewey notes that aesthetic experiences are most definitely tied to the art object that affords the experience, and the experience is valuable in and of itself. Dewey (1934: 57) notes that an object 'is peculiarly and dominantly aesthetic, yielding the enjoyment characteristic of esthetic perception, when the factors that determine anything which can be called an experience are lifted high above the threshold of perception and are made manifest for their own sake'.

This quote highlights the connection between the object perceived and the experience that arises from this imaginative engagement, as well as the value of the experience as being for its own sake rather than being used in an instrumental manner to gain some other good or goal. What is significant is that aesthetic experience is *an* experience in relation to an object or place (i.e.

an artwork, performance, or natural beauty such as a sunset or lush forest or the beach) that may result from a mode of contemplation and this experience included elements of both cognition and feeling. It also involves the imagination. Aesthetic experiences possess a phenomenological quality that includes being absorbed, focussed and open and receptive to the object under contemplation, with a curiosity and excited expectation as to what may be revealed through one's engagement with (and perception of) the object. Collinson (1992: 133) notes that 'aesthetic contemplation ... has both passive and active aspects and C. S. Lewis was surely right when he observed that 'The first demand any work of art makes on us is surrender' (Lewis, 1961: 19). But contemplation maintains a dialogue with what is perceived.' Aesthetic experiences may come upon us when we are not expecting them, but they may also emerge and are more likely to result from when we are engaging with art objects in a particular, open, contemplative and imaginative manner.

Although Eaton's definition of art differs from mine, her connection between aesthetic experience and the art object being perceived remains relevant. As Eaton (2001: 3–4) argues:

> A work of art is an artifact that is treated in aesthetically relevant ways, at least when it is being considered as a work of art, not as a doorstop or an alarm. Things are art when they are treated in such a way that someone who is fluent in a culture directs attention to an artifact's intrinsic properties that are considered worthy of attention (perception and/or reflection) within that culture. Furthermore, the person who attends to the artifact and has what he or she would describe as an aesthetic experience realizes that the experience is caused, at least in large part, because he or she is attending to intrinsic properties of the artifact considered worthy of attention in his or her community.

Thus, as we have already noted, our aesthetic experiences result from the connection between art and perception and, as such, are partly biological and partly socialised. It is a specific kind of seeing that the arts encourage. The vision adopted is one that truly *looks* and *sees*, sympathetically,[3] with an open respect for that which is being received. Art is often associated with a feeling of the sublime or of wonder, which brings with it the 'expansion of cognition' and 'intensity of perception' (Hepburn, 1980: 16). Again, while this is a natural ability we have, it is enhanced and supported through education, not solely to enhance our experiences and make us more receptive to encountering and embracing aesthetic experiences, but also to help us realize that it is artworks that may afford such experiences due to their intrinsic function or distinctive value.

Art teachers can assist students to *see* in a particular way – attending to form and specific details and 'reading' the artworks in ways that are required and invited by specific media and texts in order to glean the meaning and experience the affect that is there to be experienced.[4] This 'aesthetic literacy' is a skill set that art teachers can teach their students, enabling them to make meaning from artworks that connect to and draws upon formal, aesthetic, historical and technical knowledge and understanding of artworks, art forms and various media. Art teachers must therefore have specialist knowledge and training themselves in order to be able to support their students to learn about, for instance, art history, aesthetic theory and the technical skills involved in art making. In this respect, I agree with Maxine Greene, whose theory of aesthetic education we critically examined in the previous chapter. Yet, I see a much closer connection between aesthetic experience and ordinary experience than that which seems to be allowed for upon Greene's (2001) account.

When students create their own artworks, art teachers can guide them to hone their perception in relation to their own work as well as learn and practise the skills and techniques required in order to manifest the form they have in mind. Teachers can also role-model and assist students in learning to adopt, the open, receptive mode of perception towards artworks that is conducive to perceiving the artwork aesthetically as well as to experiencing a feeling of awe and wonder in relation to the art object. While such a mode of perception and the accompanying aesthetic experiences of the sublime or delight may well come naturally and even frequently to some, this is not to say that there is not also an important role for teachers in supporting such aesthetic literacy. Aesthetic literacy involves practising an open and receptive mode of perception; it includes engaging imaginatively with (art) objects. Such aesthetic literacy as I describe here is, I suggest, conducive to aesthetic experiences. Returning to my earlier example of *Don Giovanni*, my high school music teacher laid the groundwork that enabled me and my classmates to be moved by the opera by teaching us some formal, historical, aesthetic and technical skills and knowledge that ensured we were prepared to receive the work in an open manner, receptive to the aesthetic experience it had to offer us. The aesthetic experience was indeed felt, and shared with my classmates, and to this day, I vividly remember that lesson, the music and, most significantly, how moved I was; how we all were.

Therefore, such aesthetic experiences are a part (or extension) of our everyday experiences,[5] yet there is still a vital role for the arts and aesthetic education on the curriculum that sees art educators inducting pupils into the skills, techniques, history, theory, critique and experiences proffered by engaging with the arts. A holistic or well-rounded approach to education must include the arts and aesthetic education.

Even if we cannot directly *teach* students *how* to have an aesthetic experience, we may create the conditions conducive to such experiences (of the sublime, wonder, awe) and we may encourage students to adopt an open, receptive mode of perception that is amenable to such experiences. The arts are the ideal vehicle for prompting aesthetic experiences due to the ways in which they present concepts, images and ideas in new and creative ways. Such artistic depiction encourages those engaging with artworks to adopt a certain way of seeing – a mode of perception that is open and receptive and thus likely to result in aesthetic experiences.

In many educational spaces, the arts are more accessible than stunning natural landscapes, and artists create art objects that are intended to afford aesthetic experience; this is their distinctive purpose, thereby making them perfectly suited to such an aim. An educational curriculum without compulsory aesthetic education and a proper valuing of the arts is negligent of our aim to cultivate flourishing human beings who deserve meaningful aesthetic experiences and I shall further defend this claim with reference to Martha Nussbaum's central human capabilities framework.

Aesthetica and *eudaimonia*

Education for *eudaimonia* (flourishing) is a well rounded approach to education that is supported by many national curricula. For example, schools in England are legally required to promote the holistic development of pupils. The UK Education Act 2002 has a general requirement that the curriculum '(a) promotes the spiritual, moral, cultural, mental and physical development of pupils at the school and of society, and (b) prepares pupils at the school for the opportunities, responsibilities and experiences of later life'. Similarly, the Australian Curriculum has a set of seven general capabilities that are also intended to prepare students for life, not solely examinations. These include:

- Literacy
- Numeracy
- Information and communication technology competence
- Critical and creative thinking
- Personal and social competence

- Ethical behaviour
- Intercultural understanding.

These general capabilities 'refer to a set of knowledge, skills, behaviours and dispositions that can be developed and applied across the curriculum to help students become successful learners, confident and creative individuals and active and informed citizens' (ACARA, 2011). Formally, then, in policy documents, education is seen to aim at more than solely vocational aims (wanting students to ultimately gain employment) or academic aims (wanting students to fare well on tests and exams). Educational institutions aim at cultivating well-rounded citizens who will *do well* in the world. And this 'doing well' is akin to living a good life, whereby one is sociable and autonomous – able to participate in society and do more than simply meet one's basic needs: we want our students to grow up to flourish not simply 'survive'. Educators themselves want their students to live happy, successful lives. But these value-laden terms ('good', 'happy', 'successful') initially sound slightly vague – because of course there must be room for subjective tastes and preferences given what individuals like or are good at, but then there are also shared goods all people want and need.

The good life requires others *as well as myself* to be able to meet their basic human needs, be respected, included in communities, given opportunities to work, care, play, form relationships and be able to find personal meaning and value as they live their lives. With its roots in Ancient Greek philosophy, some elements of *eudaimonia* are to do with luck: such as being healthy, attractive, wealthy and intelligent, all of which helps one to live well. Yet other aspects are cultivated and practised, such as certain character traits (virtues) that are habituated, friendships and *phronesis* (practical wisdom) (Aristotle, 1876). There is an emphasis on rationality and reasonableness, and on recognizing that *eudaimonia* is an ongoing activity rather than a settled state one reaches. In order to flesh out what a flourishing life consists of, Martha Nussbaum's list of human capabilities (2006: 76–7) is worth mentioning here. Her ten central human capabilities are objective features of a good life that may be considered contextually in light of individual differences and social/cultural settings. It comprises:

1. Life.
2. Bodily Health.
3. Bodily Integrity – freedom of movement and freedom against violent assault.

4. Senses, Imagination and Thought.
5. Emotions. Being able to have attachments to things and people outside ourselves.
6. Practical Reason. Being able to form a conception of the good and to engage in critical reflection about the planning of one's life includes freedom of religion.
7. Affiliation.

    A. Being able to live with and towards others, to recognize and show concern for other human beings, to engage in various forms of social interaction; to be able to imagine the situation of another.

    B. Having the social bases of self-respect and non-humiliation; being able to be treated as a dignified being whose worth is equal to that of others. This entails provisions of non-discrimination on the basis of race, sex, sexual orientation, ethnicity, caste, religion, national origin.
8. Other Species. Being able to live with concern for and in relation to animals, plants and the world of nature.
9. Play. Being able to laugh, to play, to enjoy recreational activities.
10. Control over One's Environment.

    A. Political. Being able to participate effectively in political choices that govern one's life.

    B. Material. Being able to hold property (both land and movable goods), and having property rights on an equal basis with others.

It should be noted that the room for aesthetic experiences is present most obviously in capability number four 'senses, imagination, and thought', which Nussbaum (2006: 76) details as follows:

> Being able to use the senses, to imagine, think, and reason – and to do these things in a 'truly human' way, a way informed and cultivated by an adequate education, including, but by no means limited to, literacy and basic mathematical and scientific training. Being able to use imagination and thought in connection with experiencing and producing works and events of one's own choice, religious, literary, musical, and so forth. Being able to use one's mind in ways protected by guarantees of freedom of expression with respect to both political and artistic speech, and freedom of religious exercise. Being able to have pleasurable experiences and to avoid nonbeneficial pain.

Note that Nussbaum connects the fully human use of our senses and our capacity for imagination and thought to education: in order to be able to think well and truly interpret, appreciate and express ourselves in various ways, including artistically, our senses and imaginative and rational capacities must be 'informed and cultivated by an adequate education'. Society should create and support healthy, inclusive policies and institutions – including educational – conducive to flourishing. It is in supporting the capabilities outlined here that society may encourage 'fully human' lives to be led by its citizens and this includes taking care of those who may not be able to maximally experience all there is to experience or function autonomously due to their individual needs or disabilities without diminishing their human dignity.

The capability of creative, artistic expression and aesthetic appreciation and experience is connected to one of the natural functions human persons (potentially[6]) have. If we fail to realize this capacity, our expressive and experiential abilities are thus diminished and our lives less likely to flourish as a result. This is true of each of the ten central human capabilities Nussbaum details. To the extent that one does not have control over their environment or their own body, this also negatively impacts upon autonomy, life satisfaction and individual happiness. On this account, a human being flourishes to the extent that all ten capabilities are made manifest. The manifestation of these capabilities will necessarily be connected to the individual life in question: their abilities, preferences and social context (time, place and circumstance). But there is sufficient in common with the category of being human that allows a list such as this to be drawn up, and for aesthetic experience to be a component of the fourth capability listed: senses, imagination and thought.

The argument I delineated earlier in this chapter, about the instinct for art as natural, aligns with this view and supports the claim that the natural human life will include artistic expression and aesthetic experience. If this aesthetic component is missing, that life is diminished, or 'not fully human', merely animalistic, and more akin to surviving than thriving. Flourishing, or thriving, involves more than simply making ends meet or meeting basic needs. A fully human life involves meaning making and enjoyment that connects to our central human capacities.

If any of these central human capabilities are not functioning, then we are not thriving beings, we are simply living, or surviving. This connects to the capacity we have as humans to express ourselves in creative, artistic ways, to use our imagination, and perceive objects and our environment in aesthetically informed ways. Recognizing something as beautiful, and naming it as such, is an incredibly *human* thing to do. This category of 'aesthetic' names certain types of experiences we have and are capable of creating for others. To the extent that we do not recognize the beauty, wonder, sublime, artistic elements of the world in which we live, and to the extent that we are not curious about such creative endeavours to convey meaning through artistic forms and media, we are diminished as we fail to manifest our innate artistic capabilities. A life without any engagement with art (reception or creation) might be impossible, given artforms surround us, but it would also be dulled: and certainly not flourishing.

Now, it may be the case that many humans simply live or survive, or perhaps fail to meet the criteria for flourishing. However, Nussbaum's list of central human capabilities makes a moral claim about what a human being needs to live well and this is a call for justice. The list may be seen as an alternative to the universal declaration of human rights, but works in a similar way to promote real freedom and autonomy for every individual. As Robeyns and Byskov (2023) analyse:

> Nussbaum (2000: 70–7; 2006: 78–81) justifies this list by arguing that each of these capabilities is needed in order for a human life to be "not so impoverished that it is not worthy of the dignity of a human being" (2000: 72). She defends these capabilities as being the moral entitlements of every human being on earth. She formulates the list at an abstract level and advocates that the translation to implementation and policies should be done at a local level, taking into account local differences. Nussbaum argues that this list can be derived from a Rawlsian overlapping consensus and stresses that her list remains open-ended and always open for revision (Nussbaum, 2000: 77).

Thus the role for educators (along with other significant people in a child's life, including appropriate governmental agencies) to try and support children and young people to realize they are entitled to these aspects of a human life; to live well, is vital.

Many contemporary theorists support the idea of education for flourishing, even if their definitions of flourishing are slightly different from one another (Kristjánsson, 2017). Variously, flourishing is seen as autonomous, wholehearted and successful immersion in worthwhile pursuits (activities and relationships) (White, 2011); wholehearted, embodied engagement with life (Snow, 2015); a worthwhile life that contains objective goods and is 'lived from the inside' (Brighouse, 2006: 16); and Kristjánsson (2016; 2020) adds specific emotional attachments such as 'awe-inspired attractions to transpersonal ideals'. On these accounts, education and schooling *is* education for the good life, as education prepares students for a successful life as an autonomous adult in society beyond the classroom. For Kristjánsson (2020: 1), education is 'part of the good life, rather than just a preparation for it'. Most educators aim at their students thriving, not simply surviving, and in so far as this is our goal, flourishing is the aim of education.

The flourishing life includes aesthetic engagement and appreciation. In a significant way, the arts are ubiquitous and it is very difficult to completely avoid them. We are surrounded by music (every time we walk into a shop, buskers on the streets, the radio or TV playing in the background), architecture, drawings and paintings (street art, advertisements, decorations), television and technological art (social media is replete with selfies and shared images as well as tunes: we are image makers as well as consumers). We may instinctively like or dislike some of these, but there is room for education to assist us in discerning what we like (or dislike) and why and to consciously choose to seek out or surround ourselves with certain artforms. The various arts bring pleasure and meaning to people – with ample room for subjective taste and individual preferences.

If education is to prepare students for a flourishing life, it must expose students to art making and appreciation and teach them that the enjoyment the arts have to offer is an option available for them to choose to include in their lives. In order to make aesthetic experiences a readily accessible component of their lives, students must be taught how to *experience* art. This involves valuing art for its own sake: for the purpose for which it is created; namely, to evoke an aesthetic experience in the receiver of the artwork.

Imagine Frank Jackson's (1986) Mary, who grew up in a black and white room but is a brilliant scientist who knows all there is to know about colour. When Mary finally leaves the black and white room, and sees the colour red for the first time, defenders of *qualia* claim she learns something new. Something she could only learn through experience. The experience of red is not something she can explain in a reductionist or propositional manner, but it is nevertheless some form of knowledge that is significant. Mary, prior to experiencing red, was missing out on something.

Similarly, if Mary had never encountered art: experienced a beautiful melody, sung, danced, stared at an intriguing painting or paused to admire a sculpture, to that extent at least her life was lacking. Regardless of whether artworks offer us new knowledge that cannot be gleaned elsewhere,[7] it offers us distinct experiences that contribute to a life being fully human rather than merely animalistic (a distinction Nussbaum draws in 2000: 72 and 2006: 76). If we simply meet our basic needs and survive rather than thrive, then this is not living in a fully human way, and it is certainly not flourishing. Mary in the black and white room is only surviving, because she is not engaging with the social and environmental aspects of the world of which she is a part. There are several of Nussbaum's listed human capabilities that Mary appears to be missing. The flourishing life includes all of these capabilities, including aesthetic experiences, and artworks play a vital role in connecting human beings to such aesthetic experiences.

In order to form young people's capabilities, educators must introduce them to those things that are required to develop and habituate their capacities such that they may then *choose* them in adulthood.[8] As Nussbaum (2011: 152) explains, 'This formation is valuable in itself and a source of lifelong satisfaction'. Such an account defends a liberal arts tradition whereby education requires the arts and humanities to support society and individuals within societies to flourish (Nussbaum, 2010). The reason the flourishing life includes artistic expression and aesthetic experiences is because this is one of the factors which elevates our lives from simple existence and the meeting of our basic needs to having available to us the option of the fully human life; a life that is connected to our culture and creative history. This includes understanding that art exists, can be created and enjoyed, and it also includes aesthetic experiences as we have a capacity for a certain type of experience that is truly human.

As I have explained, aesthetic experience is connected to our senses, to our ability to perceive aesthetic qualities, and to interpret these, applying our cognition and emotions, and make meaning that is personal and socio-cultural as a result. The aesthetic experiences that arise when we do this are intrinsically valued and are a distinct component of the flourishing life. It is in supporting the capabilities outlined here that society may encourage 'fully human' lives to be led by its citizens, whereby 'the human being as a dignified free being who shapes his or her own life in cooperation and reciprocity with others, rather than being passively shaped or pushed around by the world' (Nussbaum, 2000: 72). This includes aesthetic experiences as a conspicuous ingredient in the well-lived life.

My argument in defence of compulsory aesthetic education on the basis of the aesthetic experiences the arts provide that are a necessary component to a flourishing life does not prevent my support for arguments defending the role (some) arts play in moral education, self-expression or the cultivation of other valuable habits. I contend that the distinctive value of engagement with art is in light of the aesthetic experience they afford. Such experiences are personally fulfilling and meaningful, they may be emotive and/or cognitive, possibly sublime, and the flourishing life includes such dynamic experiences.

Obviously, children and young people may be enjoying arts and crafts in imaginative and creative ways in their everyday lives outside of school, and we have already noted that it is impossible to entirely avoid aesthetic experiences given they may be experienced in nature or on the street. Yet there is much to be gained by supporting young people to have informed encounters with the multiple arts such that they may experience a wide range of aesthetic experiences and be open to those which truly resonate with them.

Conclusion

Education in the arts and art theory is vital. In this chapter I have detailed the crux of my argument that aesthetic education is necessary due to its ability to offer, invite and invoke aesthetic experience. Such meaningful experiences, of flow, harmony, beauty, the sublime, awe, wonder, etc., are natural and integral to a flourishing life and, therefore, educators have a responsibility to teach students that they may participate in such experiences. The arts affect everyone; they are an unavoidable part of contemporary society and have always been a part of human society from the earliest days of sharing stories, songs, the Dreamtime, cave paintings and crafts. While the arts have many roles and effects, they are uniquely created to evoke feelings (of wonder, shock, awe, the sublime and other emotions) and encourage perceivers to adopt various perspectives on an image, idea or concept. The ability to engage with the arts, particularly with high art, avant-garde art and historical art, in order to glean such experiences is more likely to succeed and be rendered more vibrant and authentic if one has been inducted into them. The aesthetic experiences that are then available to a person are unlimited.

No one should be denied the opportunity to make an informed choice as to whether or not they include the multiple arts in various ways in their lives, and everyone should be aware that they have the capability for aesthetic experience. The flourishing life includes aesthetic experiences as a source of joy, meaning making and a constructive use of one's imagination and senses. It is for these reasons that aesthetic education should be compulsory. In the next chapter I will examine some objections to my thesis and respond to those objections, thus further strengthening my argument in favour of compulsory aesthetic education for all school-aged students.

5

Objections and replies

Introduction

After having detailed my defence of aesthetic education on the basis of the vital role for aesthetic experiences in the flourishing life, I will now consider two possible objections to my defence of the necessity of aesthetic education. The first I shall call the 'naturalistic' objection, and the second I shall call the 'subjectivity' objection. The first objection is connected to the argument I have made about human persons having a natural instinct for art. If people naturally derive pleasure from the arts and nature instinctively, why do we need to educate them to receive aesthetic experiences, and the second part to this objection is why do we need to educate them in the arts (instead of anything else)? Surely the aesthetic experiences one has simply by being human and living in the world suffice to ensure our lives are happier (to the extent that we feel and encounter such aesthetic experiences)? And if we were to connect such experiences to education, why not environmental education, which seems a particularly good match for natural and accessible experiences of awe, wonder, beauty and the sublime?

The second objection is to do with individual preferences and choices involved in what the flourishing or fulfilled life should look like. If indeed there is a lot of subjectivity involved in the hobbies and forms of entertainment on which one chooses to spend one's time, energy and resources, why must this include the arts? This 'subjectivity' objection asks why the mad keen sports fan who doesn't spend any time engaging with art cannot be equally satisfied with a life filled with enjoying, watching, playing and critiquing football or tennis or car racing. Some people may simply not be very bothered by art or gain much pleasure from the arts, and certainly have no aptitude for or desire to create art, so why is their life any less full of aesthetic experiences, or even if it is, any less flourishing as a result? This objection asks why defend the centrality of aesthetic experience to the flourishing life and connect that to the arts? I shall respond to each of these objections in turn.

The naturalistic objection

Firstly, the 'naturalistic' objection. I have acknowledged that people may simply stumble upon aesthetic experiences, particularly in response to natural beauty, and this is possible because we have an innate capacity to contemplate and experience the aesthetic features of the world (natural as well as handmade). So why should aesthetic education be compulsory? Well, this could be asked of almost anything for which we educate. Just because people have the capability of being reasonable, reading, writing, kicking a football, etc., does not preclude the importance of some form of learning to support these skills and abilities and, more importantly, the education of such skills and abilities ensures they are improved.

While some people may (naturally) delight in a great many things and seemingly undergo aesthetic experiences fairly easily, this is not true of everyone, and it is certainly true that even those blessed with a propensity towards aesthetic experiences will not easily receive such responses in relation to all artworks. While nature seems to be an environment that may be well suited to spontaneous aesthetic responses in relation to natural beauty, which stimulates feelings of awe and delight, artworks are not always so readily accessible. And oftentimes the more accessible an artwork is, the less likely it is to generate an intense aesthetic response in a viewer. (Note I do not hold that this is necessarily or always true, just that currently it is a truism of much mass art. It may be less true of public artworks and performances, and it may well change over time as, for instance, televisual narrative artworks are constantly improving and diversifying on account of ever-developing technological abilities and rising consumer demand.)

Given that not everyone has immediate access to beautiful or picturesque, or staggering and awesome natural landscapes – certainly not in their daily lives – artworks seem like a good place to look to for aesthetic experience. Artworks are intentionally created in order to produce aesthetic experiences in their viewers and may be steadily contemplated as a means of achieving this affect. Artworks may not always result in such a moving, potentially transformative, aesthetic experience, but the tripartite features that may lead to such experiences include the skill (the technique, the vision, the ability) of the artist to create an art object with relevant (formal) features, the display and presentation of the work which includes contextual elements (it may be advisable to ask who is the assumed audience) and, thirdly, the attitude of the person engaging with or receiving the work. The manner in which a person approaches an artwork is of vital significance in relation to how they experience it. As we saw in Chapter 3, Maxine Greene spends much time explaining how arts educators must teach their students *how* to see, and she also claims that artworks train people to *see differently*. There is something important here about the attention paid – attention paid to detail, to the subtle features that comprise an artwork – that allows one to truly understand and appreciate it. This kind of looking, and paying close attention requires practice, and often takes time.

If we need to slow down and attend to an artwork (or a natural landscape) in order to appreciate it, understand it, and allow a related feeling to arise in response, these preconditions of many aesthetic experiences do indeed need to be cultivated, habituated and role-modelled. Again, this is not to rule out the fact that all of this may occur spontaneously – and of course it does – but in busy lives full of many things to do and see, we may well need reminding of how to be receptive to such aesthetic experiences. What I am suggesting here is that it would be advisable for young people (all people, really, but it is a good idea to start early!) to learn and practise such techniques so that they are then equipped with such skills. If we practise being receptive and appropriately attentive to the beauty in life, we develop and hopefully retain this ability.

It may very well be that as we get older and have busy lives replete with responsibilities, we are perhaps slightly less surprised by life – less open to being delighted and to laughing, to receiving the beauty and joy the world and especially artworks have to offer, as routine and mundane tasks and habits pull at our attention in a familiar way. It is here that these habits of attending to what is beautiful or surprising and novel in life could stand us in good stead to experience aesthetic moments in response to objects in the world. Furthermore, such habits may then encourage us to seek these moments out and specifically look for the wondrous moments that artworks (and nature) offer.

It seems right that, particularly as one grows up, one is more likely to enjoy the artistic activity if they are *better* at it – either better at producing the artworks in question, having the requisite skills to be able to express what they have in mind, or better at understanding and interpreting what it is they are experiencing via the artwork with which they engage. It would get frustrating to continue to not quite grasp or 'fail' at being able to create the sort of thing you want to as you get older once you have spent some time, effort and energy on the arts. Greene discusses the unique pleasure people seek to derive from works of art but are often unable to realize due to their lack of adequate knowledge and skill. She takes the goal of aesthetic education to be the development of aesthetic literacy, which she defines simply (and unhelpfully if the educator seeks to translate this into concrete curriculum and lesson planning) as the capacity to unlock the inherent values of works of art (1978: 171).

When we understand and appreciate the artwork and the creative process in question, we are enjoying a 'worthwhile activity'. Worthwhile activities are necessary components of a flourishing life. John White (2011: 59) points out that for an activity to be worthwhile it must have some intrinsic value and be good to do for its own sake. Wellbeing requires successful engagement in worthwhile activities. While White uses the word 'fail' to denote activities or hobbies we may attempt but not succeed in, and this may well apply to creative endeavours, I prefer the idea of cultivation. We cultivate the habits, techniques and attentive mode of reception required to help us achieve a sense of satisfaction in relation to the pursuit we are undertaking. We may do this on our own, but we are often well guided and supported by mentors and teachers or others with relevant experience in that particular activity.

Creative pursuits often involve trying and trying again, trying something new and then a different technique, in order to eventually achieve the final product or to understand a particular poem. Occasionally artists speak about how the final version does not look as they had originally imagined or intended, or how they may not have a fixed final idea in mind to start with but rather followed the creative process where it leads. This process, which may depend somewhat on the art media and style under discussion, requires trust in one's cultivated skills and techniques alongside adaptability in order to still create an artwork as a 'successful' end result. It also requires determination and patience – further virtuous traits that require cultivation, habituation and practice.

However, the initial point still stands: if I do not have the patience to develop particular artistic skills required to pursue a certain activity, I may not stick with it. This seems to be truer in adulthood, usually as additional demands on our time mean that we end up selecting fewer rather than additional activities, pastimes, or career options. I can certainly imagine people – especially young people and children – enjoying singing, making music, dancing, and painting even if they are not very skilled or accomplished at it, but I am more likely to continue dedicating time, effort, energy and resources into something that I not only enjoy but can also understand or express myself in the way I wish. In fact, much enjoyment is likely predicated on being able to understand (i.e. the artwork in question or how the technique used creates a certain affect) and achieve an end result that pleases its creator.

White gives examples of hobbies and other accomplishments that may make up a successful life that, along with other features, might well be described as a flourishing life. Some of these additional features include mood and temperament – for instance, the depressed person, even if successful may not be flourishing if everything takes a lot of effort and they do not seem to enjoy the things they do or accomplish as a result of their mental state. A fulfilled life, White claims, also requires autonomy, determination, whole-heartedness and courage (2011: 61). I am more likely to enjoy the artistic activity I am engaged in (art making or receiving) if I understand it or have a reasonable chance of creating something that resembles what I aim to construct. I add that engaging in an artwork such that the resulting experience is beautiful, moving, meaningful, or even shocking – that is to say, it is an aesthetic experience – comes from engaging in what R. S. Peters (1966) calls a worthwhile activity; it is enjoyed for its own sake. I would add that such artistic worthwhile activities are enjoyed for the sake of the experience they offer – namely those aesthetic experiences I have defended as imperative to the flourishing life. Note that I am not claiming that all such successful or enjoyable engagement with the arts will result in aesthetic experiences, yet these features are supportive of such experiences. As has already been explored in Chapters 2 and 4, these aesthetic experiences are demarcated from the everyday, ordinary, banal or mundane. They are a component of the flourishing or fulfilled life – a life that is elevated above simply existing; a life that is truly human.

The benefit of aesthetic education is that it introduces people to many more kinds of aesthetic experience, and many diverse artforms. It also supports art making, as well as critiquing and contextualizing artworks, which further enhances the experiential aspect of engaging with artworks. Art teachers are able to do this by making additional understanding, frameworks and meaning available to young people through scaffolded lessons. By teaching and role modelling specific artistic and aesthetic techniques (to do with art making, crafting, viewer engagement and critique, history and theory), art teachers are an invaluable resource for young people to learn that there is so much they may engage with aesthetically, and they may create their own artworks from which they and others may also derive aesthetic experiences. This hard-earned joy (as learning to create satisfactory artworks is difficult and artistic skills require a lot of work, patience and practice) adds to the flourishing life.

This does not preclude environmental education being useful in the same way: to enhance one's receptivity towards nature and engender aesthetic experiences. However, sublime natural beauty is less accessible for many schools in urban areas and environmental education is often connected to issues of sustainability, scientific understanding and ethics. Particularly given the climate crisis and its associated environmental impacts, the focus of environmental education is only partially dedicated to enjoying nature and, as such, it is not as well suited to our purposes as art and aesthetic education. A separate defence of environmental education is required, I think, and enjoying aesthetic experiences is a part of that defence, for sure. However, I don't think it is the central argument in favour of environmental education, even if environmental education may also help increase young people's experiences of awe, wonder and the sublime.

There is no problem for my argument by adding that we should also encourage people to gain more aesthetic experiences from enjoying nature. The flourishing life is made up of many components, including aesthetic experiences derived from nature and the arts. Happily, it is a case of 'the more the merrier'! However, learning to appreciate the aesthetic aspects of our environment, which includes natural, found objects and handmade artworks, takes place in art classes. Thus, I focus on the arts because they are specifically created to intentionally produce an aesthetic experience. And art teachers intentionally cultivate in students their ability to notice, appreciate and create artistic forms. This education and cultivation makes it much more likely that people will attend to and enjoy the aesthetic experiences available to them – whether they are in nature, in an art gallery, online or in the street.

Thus, while I claim human beings do have the natural predisposition to undergo aesthetic experiences on the basis of their perceptive organs and ability to imagine, feel and construct meaning from all they see, hear, touch, taste, speak (or sing) and move, this ability is greatly enhanced when it is guided in its development. This is particularly true in relation to artworks and artistic creations. Here the role for the formal or informal arts educator is vital (even if one is self-taught they have likely made use of resources such as books or online sources that act as guides and teachers). And the case for engaging with artworks is strong given that such objects are uniquely created with the intention of producing an aesthetic experience in their viewers and there is always 'something for everyone' – some artform or object that particularly moves a person. While there may be other reasons to create art – such as practical reasons including in order to earn a living – the central reason, which is necessary and ensures an art object is essentially an artwork *qua* Art, is that it is designed to be experienced for its own sake alone. This amounts to experiencing the artwork for the sake of the experience it affords – namely, an aesthetic experience, which counts as a worthwhile activity.

The ability to enjoy aesthetic experiences *must* be a natural predisposition if it is to be a feature of the flourishing human life on my conception. And this allows for people of various levels of ableness and understanding to enjoy and appreciate the multiple and various arts in ways that suit their needs and capabilities. But just because aesthetic experiences are *natural* does not mean that our ability to access such experiences is not guided, taught, encouraged and usefully enhanced by a relationship with a teacher, formal or informal, particularly in relation to artworks. Narrative artworks at a bare minimum usually require an understanding of language, for instance. And there is so much more to enjoy, learn, experience and undergo when artworks and their related techniques, skill sets and artistic devices are imparted. It is such skills, techniques and an understanding of the same that may enhance and ultimately allow one to experience an aesthetic experience in relation to the art object in question, or to produce such a response in others who engage with the artworks one has designed.

Aesthetic education, then, is ideally suited to stimulate an openness to aesthetic features, art objects, and help cultivate the attentiveness required in order to maximize one's chance of artistic pursuits affording aesthetic experiences. This is so precisely because art making and receiving is a worthwhile activity aimed entirely at promoting the aesthetic (this includes 'beauty', but it is wider than beauty alone). While we all have a natural predisposition to be able to undergo such aesthetic experiences, we are more likely to have such experiences and have them in relation to a wider set of stimuli if we are educated in the skills and knowledge associated with the multiple and varied arts.

The subjectivity objection

Secondly, the 'subjectivity' objection. For those theorists who do defend inclusion of the arts on the curriculum as a component of the flourishing life, most of them defend it as an option for students to choose rather than as a compulsory subject. When listing specific educational goods and capacities, for instance, Brighouse et al. (2018: 27) identify: capacity for economic productivity; capacity for personal autonomy; capacity for democratic competence; capacity for healthy personal relationships; capacity to treat others as equals and the capacity for personal fulfilment. While all six capacities contribute to flourishing lives, the space for arts education is within the capacity for personal fulfilment as one amongst a number of options available to people. The authors write:

> Healthy personal relationships are important for flourishing, but so too are complex and satisfying labor and projects that engage one's physical, aesthetic,

intellectual, and spiritual faculties. People find great satisfaction in music, literature, and the arts; games and sports; mathematics and science; and religious practice. In these and other activities, they exercise and develop their talents and meet challenges ... School is a place in which children's horizons can be broadened. They can be exposed to – and can develop enthusiasms for and competence in – activities that they would never have encountered through familial and communal networks and that sometimes suit them better than any they would have encountered in those ways. The capacity to find joy and fulfillment from experiences and activities is at the heart of a flourishing life.

(Brighouse et al., 2018: 26–7)

Similarly, Reiss and White (2013) see the importance of offering students various, diverse experiences that they may or may not stumble across elsewhere, so that individuals may ascertain whether they have the skill, passion, talent, or enjoyment of that activity that could lead to personal meaning making and fulfilment. As White (2011: 65) notes, 'directly, then, or indirectly via the imagination, families and schools will induct children into all sorts of worthwhile activities and relationships.' These defences suffice to justify the inclusion of the arts on the curriculum as an option that students can try and select more of if they enjoy and/or possess the requisite talent. But, as is noticeable on Brighouse et al.'s account of personal fulfilment, if someone prefers to play sport or enjoy nature or solve maths equations, these activities could suffice for their flourishing lives without the requirement that they also engage in art making and reception.

The arguments offered by Brighouse et al., and Reiss and White certainly support my case in favour of aesthetic education, yet I wish to further justify and substantiate the claim that *all* school-aged students should be taught the skills and techniques of art making, appreciation and art theory due to its distinctive aesthetic value. Meaningful activities, from which individuals choose what they wish to do, of which painting, dancing, writing or acting may be one option, only suggest students should be exposed to these things in case they wish to choose the activity in question. Yet *every* student will benefit from being exposed to and taught how to appreciate aesthetic experiences. This defends aesthetic education: of which arts making and creating is one aspect, and learning to engage with artworks is another, the latter of which includes a theoretical element alongside the practical skill of learning artistic techniques.

Let us consider the example of the mad keen sports fan who is not interested in any arts. Of this person I initially want to ask whether they have ever been properly introduced to the arts in their younger years? They may very well be enjoying aesthetic elements of the 'beautiful game' as well as the competition, comradery and feeling a sense of belonging to a team. They sing songs and chant and drum, they dress up in their team colours and decorate themselves and their surroundings to match, they appreciate the movement and skill of the players … It does not seem unlikely that they would also find enjoyment in music, dance and theatre!

An argument along John Stuart Mill's lines would argue that (some) arts would offer higher-order pleasures than (some) sports (Mill, 1861: II 5). The idea of some pleasures being of a higher quality (those with cognitive components, and achievements one has to work for) rather than sensuous and fleeting pleasures has been charged with elitism. I do not wish to make use of this hierarchical ladder of 'lower' or 'higher' pleasures and I do not want to pit football against ballet, or tennis against opera. Instead, I would argue that where one has a narrow set of aesthetic experiences, they could be widened to include more and those who stick to only one kind of entertainment are missing out on others.

For the adult who chooses only to engage with sports, the ingrained habit and associated lifestyle is difficult (though not impossible) to alter. And, yes, they may indeed be very happy (in a self-described manner). However, for children and young people, this is the prime moment to offer them additional opportunities which expand the options and range of choices they have before them. It is the optimistic and idealistic hope that schools may play this role for children, especially if they are not accessing such experiences or education elsewhere. Obviously, this argument applies to many aspects of education, including to career options and other lifestyle choices. But it equally and powerfully applies to the arts and to the types of aesthetic experiences that are available for young people to explore and with which they may experiment.

Returning to the defence that rests upon human capabilities, people have this capacity for aesthetic experiences, and they may choose to what extent and in what manner they do (or do not) fulfil these. Educators have a duty to provide young people with the information and experiences they need to recognize their capacities and guide them in ways that enable constructive and creative means of fulfilling these. The arts provide multiple opportunities for young people to engage their capacities with respect to the *senses, imagination and thought*, with formal and informal education – including aesthetic education – as necessary for the *fully human* use of our senses and imagination.

For those whose cultural diet consists solely of Reality television programmes, for the mad keen sports fan described above, and more drastically for Mary in her black and white room, they are missing out on other artforms whose artistic expressions could give rise to wonderful, moving and meaningful aesthetic experiences. It is more difficult to say the same of the person whose only engagement with the arts is with ballet because the ballet includes movement, theatrical expression, symphonic music and skilful costume and set design. There is more here to delight the senses and activate an aesthetic experience. And it may be that more education is required to access the aesthetic experiences associated with additional artforms, but that is not an impediment to my argument; rather, it offers further support for the importance of educating every student in the arts such that they may be open to and access additional aesthetic experiences as a result. Compulsory aesthetic education teaches *all* students that the experiences available through the multiple and various arts are there *for them* to participate in.

In fact, elsewhere, White (2011: 24) defends the arts as offering a universal source of enjoyment and personal fulfilment. And Reiss and White (2013: 20) make a compelling argument for how teaching the arts can further ensure students have the chance to understand what artworks offer in terms of their value and connection to our lives:

> Experiencing the more subtle and exquisite delights of these areas is helped enormously by induction into them by experts. People introduced to their various forms and genres tend in adult life to prize this kind of activity as part of what makes their life worth living. Like verbal arts – but more tacitly, through sound and sight and touch – these have the power of constantly reconnecting us with background thoughts and feelings about the strangeness and fleetingness of our being in the world. It is because these arts are so central to our flourishing that there should be a substantial place for them on a compulsory basis. This is compatible, of course, with optional classes in the particular arts, within this system.

Here we see Reiss and White push their defence of the arts further. They justify the inclusion of *good* literature on the curriculum for its educational qualities *and* affording *everyone* an intrinsically valuable activity, stating, 'As an activity pursued for its own sake, reading literature scores well, then, as a contributor to a flourishing life' (2013: 18). Further:

> Literature is important to all of us, partly because of its role in helping us to form a background of understanding. It can not only fill out our appreciation of our shared human nature, including its relation to the rest of nature and the universe, but it also invites us to take pleasure in reflecting about this. This is inseparable from reflectiveness about our own and other people's values, about their priorities, and conflicts between them as our life unfolds.
>
> (Reiss and White, 2013: 17)

Some of this defence of good literature (as opposed to 'Pulp fiction, soap operas, and B movies' which may be enjoyable but less educational[1]) reminds us of the arguments about the role for narrative art in moral education that were critically explored in Chapter 2. Nussbaum also defends reading good literature as a moral act and argues 'certain novels are, irreplaceably, works of moral philosophy. But I shall go further ... the novel can be a paradigm of moral activity' (Nussbaum, 1990: 148). It seems as though the intrinsic value of the act of reading good literature and of 'wholehearted and successful engagement' with other art forms is based on personal enjoyment and fulfilment which includes this moral activity – a cultivation of one's moral sensibility. And in this way Reiss and White offer a composite argument of sorts, much as we saw in Chapter 3 proposed by Eisner and Greene.

Reiss and White's composite argument here may be presented because the flourishing life is complex, subtle and, to some degree, subjective.[2] So, we find them detailing a defence of compulsory arts education due to the worthiness of the activities themselves, while also claiming that such activities are required for a flourishing life, but there is an additional component of the meaningfulness of engagement of this kind, namely, that it assists us to understand ourselves and others in the world. This understanding is connected to moral education, and it is this argument as a whole that is taken to justify making arts education compulsory.

One aspect where my argument departs from that of Reiss and White is in the justification provided for the claim that, for instance in the example of reading literature, this activity is deemed to be intrinsically valuable. Their claim of the intrinsic value of artworks seems to be connected to the line of defence of worthwhile activities which are enjoyed for their own sake. Firstly, defending aesthetic experience as intrinsically valuable is difficult, and such claims are often stated rather than explained. For instance, William Frankena (1973: 87–8) classically details a comprehensive list of intrinsic goods that includes pleasures and satisfactions; happiness; beauty, harmony, proportion in objects contemplated; aesthetic experience; and self-expression. But criteria are not provided to explain what make these things intrinsically valuable.

Further, Reiss and White count such intrinsically valuable activities as featuring in a fulfilled or flourishing life. They then also note that these activities have additional instrumental value – such as fine works of literature's capacity for moral education. Now, the arts may have both intrinsic and extrinsic values; this need not be contradictory. But there is a question as to which benefits confer their requisite status within the flourishing life. In contrast, in my argument, I explain that it is the aesthetic experiences gained from engaging with artworks that render them innately valuable and it is these experiences that are constitutive of the flourishing life. If Reiss and White intend that it is pleasure that earns artworks a place in the good life, then if one does not find any artworks pleasurable, they need not be included in the good life.

For me, aesthetic education must be compulsory rather than optional because otherwise there will be students who do not choose to learn more about the arts, probably because they do not realize how rewarding the arts can be, and this closes off or at least diminishes the opportunity for them to understand that the arts entail access to aesthetic experiences which enrich one's life. Such a diminishing or a closing off of these experiences is significant precisely due to the role aesthetic experience plays in a flourishing life, and the capacity of the arts to engender such experiences.

For Reiss and White, an education in the arts ought to be compulsory because they bring pleasure to people and may enhance their understanding of the world in which we live. If students are not inducted into the arts, they will not realize they can gain pleasure and personal meaning making from them. Now, while this may be true in some, many, or even most cases, not all artworks lend themselves to pleasurable experiences: note that the aesthetic experience is much broader and more diverse than pleasure alone. And, on my analysis, as we shall explore further in the next chapter, instrumental justification of the arts and of arts education should always be supplementary rather than central to the defence of aesthetic education.

Plus, we may note that Reiss and White defend this argument in relation to literature, illustrating their claims with convincing examples, but later add, 'To go back to more traditional curriculum activities that should be compulsory, enjoying non-literary arts – paintings, sculpture, architecture, film, music, dance – shares many of the same features as engagement in literature' (2013: 20). Yet while some artworks connect us to the world in which we find ourselves, the aesthetic experience associated with other art objects may take us away from the banality of reality. Not all artworks have moral meaning (as we, along with Nussbaum, have already noted in Chapter 2), and thus the intrinsic value of wholehearted engagement with such artworks cannot always be that it helps us understand the world even if it sometimes or often does, and even if we experience pleasure and/or personal meaning as a result of such engagement.

Even if Reiss and White do successfully justify the statutory inclusion of (good) literature on the curriculum, the necessity to read already offers a justification for the very same. Plus this justification does not easily extend to art-making, even if it can apply to some other artforms. For these reasons, I take a different tack and while Reiss and White offer a defence of compulsory arts education due to the worthiness of the activities themselves, and, in particular, their *educational* worthiness which contributes to the flourishing life, my argument rests upon the aesthetic experiences artworks afford.

It is aesthetic experiences, that admittedly are not solely gleaned through engagement with the arts, but for which the arts are an ideal source, that are necessitated by the fulfilled life. Educators have an obligation to introduce children and young people to those elements within their control that may be selected for inclusion in adult life. This includes the arts, which are the conduits for aesthetic experiences, to which each and every student should be taught are there for them to engage with, create, critique and experience. Thus, aesthetic education should be compulsory for all school-aged students, but by the time one is an adult, autonomy prevails, and people select those things they do or do not include in their lives. Adults are more likely to choose to include the arts in their lives if they have some experience, understanding and grounding in them such as that which can be provided by compulsory aesthetic education during school when they are young.

Therefore, my argument in defence of compulsory aesthetic education on the basis of the aesthetic experiences the arts provide, that are a necessary component to a flourishing life, fares better than that of Reiss and White or Brighouse et al. The line of defence I have detailed does not prevent my support for arguments defending the role (some) arts play in moral education, self-expression or the cultivation of other valuable habits, as was discussed further in Chapter 2. Nevertheless, I contend that the distinctive value of engagement with art is in light of the aesthetic experience they afford.

Such experiences are open to every one of us because we are human persons *qua* human beings with certain psychophysical features that enable us to appreciate the arts and attend to them in specific ways that are personally fulfilling and meaningful. As such, compulsory aesthetic education provides people, starting at a young age, with the knowledge (including know-how) and understanding that is needed to pursue and undergo such aesthetic experiences, and to create artworks that afford such experiences to others. These aesthetic experiences may be emotive and/or cognitive, possibly sublime, and the flourishing life includes such dynamic experiences. As educators, we must do what we can to ultimately support autonomous adults to willingly choose the components of their good life.

Conclusion

This chapter considered two possible objections to my claim that all children and young people should be taught aesthetic education as a necessary component on the school curriculum. The first objection, which I named the 'naturalistic' objection, took aim at my claim that human persons have a natural instinct for art. If people will naturally enjoy aesthetic experiences, then why should we educate for these, and why should we educate for these aesthetic experiences in the arts? The second objection, which I named the 'subjectivity' objection, challenges that engagement with the arts should be up to the individual and a matter of choice rather than compulsion. If people enjoy the arts, they should be able to select it as an option without it being statutory.

My replies to these two objections serve to further support my argument for the necessity of aesthetic education. All people are naturally predisposed to undergo aesthetic experiences, and these experiences are manifest in a flourishing life. It is precisely for this reason that we ought to teach people, starting from an early age, that they may participate in and seek out such wondrous, shocking, delightful, awe-inspiring and sublime experiences, and equip them with the knowledge, skills and awareness required to be receptive to and welcome such experiences into their lives. Such knowledge, skills and techniques may also produce in people the desire and ability to create artworks that are, in turn, capable of affecting similarly aesthetic experiences in others. Significantly, statutory aesthetic education encapsulates the value of such worthwhile activities, activities that are composite in the fulfilled life on the grounds of the experiences they afford.

Furthermore, where one only has a narrow set of aesthetic experiences, they could be widened to include more, and those who stick to only one kind of entertainment are missing out on others. For the person whose cultural diet consists solely of sports, they are missing out on artforms whose artistic expressions could give rise to wonderful, moving and meaningful aesthetic experiences. Therefore, teachers have a duty to expose young people to as many artforms as possible and teach them to engage appropriately with them so that they have the possibility of appreciating and receiving aesthetic experiences from a wide variety of sources as a result. In this way, after they grow up, these people have the opportunity of real choice: of being able to select those activities and hobbies that will be rewarding for them and know that the multiple and various arts are a viable option for them – for their aesthetic reception and creation. In this way the arts may yield more moments of aesthetic enjoyment that augments their lives.

The flourishing life includes experiences that delight the senses and activate an aesthetic experience, and compulsory aesthetic education is required to introduce and cultivate the capacity for accessing the aesthetic experiences associated with diverse artforms, particularly the artforms that are not immediately accessible on first engagement. The importance of educating every student in the arts such that they may be open to and access more aesthetic experiences as a result is precisely so that the student may develop capacities required in the flourishing life and they may then, in later years, choose to fulfil those capacities in ways that nourish and nurture *eudaimonia*.

Therefore, my argument in defence of compulsory aesthetic education on the basis of the aesthetic experiences the arts provide prioritizes the distinctive value of engagement (creation and reception) with art in light of the place for aesthetic experience in the flourishing life. In the previous chapter, I supported this argument with reference to the human capabilities model where I connected the human instinct for art and aesthetic experience to the capacity for sensing, imagination and thought. Such experiences are personally fulfilling and meaningful, they may be emotive and/or cognitive, possibly awe-filled and sublime, and the flourishing life includes such dynamic experiences.

Obviously, children and young people may be enjoying arts and crafts in imaginative and creative ways in their everyday lives outside of school, and as previously noted, it is impossible to entirely avoid aesthetic experiences given they may be experienced in nature or on the street. Yet there is much to be gained by supporting young people to have informed encounters with the multiple arts such that they may experience a wide range of aesthetic experiences and be open to those which truly resonate with them. In fact, we are doing children and young people a disservice if we do not introduce them to the arts in a way that opens up the opportunities for them to encounter aesthetic experiences, recognize them as such, value them, and go on to seek them out in their endeavours to cultivate their own good lives. In the next chapter, I will examine in closer detail what may be said about the instrumental value(s) of the arts and aesthetic education in order to ascertain whether an instrumental defence helps or hinders advocates of the arts and arts educationalists.

6

Instrumental defences of arts education

Introduction

When we refer to the value of art, and of arts education, there is an uneasiness about referring to any instrumental benefits or extrinsic value(s). There is a staunch tradition within aesthetics whereby philosophers and art theorists, artists and defenders of the arts seek to defend artworks and the value of art in an intrinsic or essentialist manner, arguing that the arts are valuable in and of themselves. Many such aesthetes have taken the stance that furthermore artworks should *only* be valued for their own sake, and not for the sake of anything else. Historically, this attitude has even excluded moral value and made it difficult to make a moral judgement of artworks, or one that might impact in some way upon the overall aesthetic judgement of that work (see D'Olimpio, 2020a). In the next chapter I will look in further detail at how we might, as educators, consider issues to do with aesthetics and ethics, particularly with social justice and matters of equity and inclusion in mind. But firstly, in this chapter, I will consider the resistance to and worry about instrumentalization, and whether any instrumental arguments that locate extrinsic value in artworks and arts education are useful, desirable and supportive of my main aim in this book, which is to defend (compulsory) aesthetic education.

I have, of course, offered a defence of aesthetic education that connects to what I have justified as the distinctive value of artworks, which is their capacity to generate aesthetic experiences. In Chapter 4, I explicitly and robustly defend my claim that the arts are specifically designed to generate aesthetic experiences for their audience, and this is a functional argument. This definition of art sees the value of the art object as intrinsic: we engage with or create and enjoy the artwork for its own sake, for the sake of the experience it affords, rather than for the sake of anything else. It may be that I can make a living as an artist and that is the way I wish to spend my time and where I seek to devote my efforts and energy, but I enjoy the making of art and the reception of artworks because they are worthwhile activities in their own right.

It is the aesthetic experience which is intrinsically valuable and worthwhile, and I then go on to argue that such aesthetic experiences are necessary to the flourishing life because they are constitutive of *eudaimonia*. The educational aspect of my argument connects to the claim that we as educators wish to prepare our students for a meaningful, satisfactory life, at best a flourishing life, which is one that includes such wondrous aesthetic experiences (among other things). Therefore, in order to teach young people that they are able to seek out and undergo such incredible experiences, ones that augment one's life, we ought to teach them the arts and the associated ways they may access such creative experiences and create such satisfying experiences for others (as art-makers) if they so desire. The educational aspect of this argument is important because while young people may naturally stumble upon arts and crafts, making and appreciating the multiple arts require a specific skill set – a skill set that is best cultivated, supported and encouraged by being taught and learned as well as practised.

This argument says that we should enjoy artworks for their distinctive offering or function: to create amazing experiences we will enjoy. Such aesthetic experiences are emergent rather than extrinsic: the experiences cannot exist without the artwork from which they are made manifest. This also means that there is an appropriate manner of engaging with the artworks in order to access these experiences, in the sense that if one is simply fantasizing, rather than imaginatively engaging with a specific artwork, then it may not be *this* particular artwork that leads to the aesthetic experience in question. In fact, this may be one way we distinguish art – including sensual artworks and erotic artworks – from pornography, for instance.

People need to learn *how* to engage appropriately with art in such a way as to be able to glean meaning and aesthetic experience(s) from artworks. This is not to say that this is the *only* way people can and do and should engage with art – but educationally it is vital that we teach people that they have this capacity for aesthetic enjoyment. It is important that we start when children are young and offer them amazing experiences that connect such aesthetic experiences to art making and reception so that they may go on to consciously choose to include art in various ways in their lives as they grow up. Making the connection between such aesthetic experiences and the arts, along with their associated meaning making and creative self-expression, is such a vital offering we as educators can provide to all children and young people. This is particularly important in case these individuals do not get such dedicated artistic and aesthetic exposure elsewhere.

So, the first half of my argument is that we ought to value artworks for the experiences they afford and the meaning making that is emergent or resultant from (appropriate) engagement with such works. Aesthetic experiences are intrinsically worthwhile and valuable to us, due to the kinds of beings we are. Thus, the second part of my argument for teaching the arts and for aesthetic education follows – that such experiences are a part of a flourishing life, to which everyone is entitled. And, as virtue ethicists will note, this is a teleological claim; it is aiming at a goal. If the (reasonable and ultimate) aim of life is *eudaimonia* – flourishing, and aesthetic experiences are one aspect of the good and pleasurable life, and we are aiming at education that equips students with the tools and skills (and character traits) required to be able to live a good life, or to be able to choose to live a good life – then we are educating for flourishing, and aesthetic education is constitutive of this goal. In this way I offer a non-instrumental defence of the arts, of aesthetic experiences and of aesthetic education.

I think it is important to acknowledge and recognize the suspicion over instrumental arguments when it comes to defending the arts and arts education. There is a long-held wariness of and hostility to defending the arts in terms of extrinsic benefits or in instrumental or utilitarian terms. In this chapter I will consider and further examine what is the cause for concern here? Why worry about art being used for an end that is extrinsic to the art object and why worry that arts education is being used for some other purpose than simply providing aesthetic experiences for students? I do want to endorse a vigilance against reductively instrumentalist arguments whereby the arts or education gets used in either a very narrowly utilitarian sense or for worrying or destructive purposes. Plus, we must be mindful of the potential for the slippery slope argument to manifest if we allow for instrumental justifications of the arts, education or arts education.

But ultimately I will suggest that not *all* instrumental arguments are to be rejected. Some forms of instrumental arguments may well allow for expansive and subtle understandings of the benefits of the arts and of education, but these must be accounted for in a transparent manner. And ultimately I contend that such arguments should be working in tandem or in addition to an essentialist defence of the arts and aesthetic education, much like the one I have provided. But I shall start by firstly considering the worthwhileness of arts education, and then I will move to consider why there is a general wariness and even open hostility towards instrumental arguments in the arts and in education.

Worthwhile activities

It has been made clear that I defend the arts based on the intrinsic value and worthwhileness of creating and receiving artworks. Now if I were to only defend arts education on the basis of the intrinsic worthwhileness of the activities themselves – namely, the intrinsic value of engaging with the arts and creating artworks – then I might have a difficult time proving that this is a subject which must necessarily be included on the curriculum. This is because there are many intrinsically worthwhile and valuable activities in our lives and we need a way to choose between them in order to defend their inclusion on the curriculum.

Hence I draw upon the premise that we as human beings seek to live the good and meaningful – flourishing – life (*eudaimonia*), and education is one important way we prepare children and young people to partake in such meaningful lives. Schooling is one of the ways by which society equips people with the means, skills, virtues, attributes, knowledge and understanding required to be autonomous adults who choose the lives they want to lead. Schools should also (ideally) provide the environment and routines that help cultivate and habituate the kinds of practical habits (practical wisdom – *phronesis*) that are required by the good life.

On this view then, aesthetic experiences, I have argued, are constitutive of the good life and best able to be (more) easily experienced and accessed in relation to multiple objects and experiences – especially artworks – if initiated. When considering young people attending school, such initiation takes place in an art classroom by an art teacher in the classroom space. The subject of 'the arts' on the curriculum thus provides these people the opportunity to realize that they may access such aesthetic experiences in relation to art – and create them for others via art media – and this is a viable option available to them.

R. S. Peters' 'non-instrumental attitude'

In his work, especially in *Ethics and Education* (1966), R. S. Peters claims we should not accept any instrumental defences of education. He himself seeks to defend education as intrinsically worthwhile, and to this end he offers his hedonistic and transcendental arguments to justify education – which he equates to theoretical and academic subjects and the academic curriculum. He sees such activities as endlessly absorbing, pleasurable, stimulating, generative and aimed at the truth. For now I shall set aside Peters' own conception and defence of education as particularly academic and theoretical, and I shall also set aside the many criticisms that have been levelled at his arguments. What I wish to focus on, however, is his concern about instrumental defences of education.

R. S. Peters, in his justification of education (1973: 241), notes:

> In contrast, too, to the instrumentality so often associated with specialized knowledge, the educated person is one who is capable, to a certain extent, of doing and knowing things for their own sake. He can delight in what he is doing without always asking the question "And where is this going to get me?" This applies as much to cooking as it does to chemistry. He can enjoy the company of a friend as well as a concert. And his work is not just a chore to be carried out for cash. He has a sense of standards as well as a sense of the setting of what he is doing between the past and the future. There are continuities in his life which reflect what he cares about. He takes care because he cares.

Further along in this same text, Peters (1973: 242–3) notes the tendency of society to value things instrumentally, including the arts and education. He says:

> The most all-pervading type of justification for anything in our type of society is to look for its use either to the community or to the individual; for basically our society is geared to consumption. Even the work of the artist, for instance, is not always valued for the excellences which are intrinsic to it. Rather it is valued because it attracts more people to a public place, because it provides a soothing or restful atmosphere for people who are exposed to it, or because of the prestige of the artist which rubs off on to the body which commissions him. Music is piped into railway stations and air terminals to make people cheerful just as heat is piped through radiators to make them warm. Art and music can be thought of in this way irrespective of how the artists or musicians conceive of what they are doing. The same sort of thing can happen to education …

It must be noted that by the time he writes 'The Justification of Education' (1973) Peters concedes that 'a strong instrumental case can also be made for the passing on of knowledge and understanding' (p. 243). He acknowledges that whatever the intrinsic benefits of education are, of knowledge, skills and understanding, it is obvious that they are necessary to the civilized community. Communication is vital and so therefore some form of education is required for people to be able to communicate, and breadth of understanding is also important to social understanding. Yet he believes any instrumental defence still needs to be supplemented by an intrinsic defence such as the worthwhileness of these activities and their place in a worthwhile life (see Hand, 2010, for a further discussion of this position). Furthermore, understanding that things can and should be valued in non-instrumental ways was itself important to Peters. He saw the education of this 'non-instrumental attitude' as vital.

Peters notes that it is difficult to explain exactly why the 'non-instrumental attitude' is important, or what is involved in this attitude. He explains that 'the key to it is that regard, respect, or love should be shown for the intrinsic features of activities' (1973: 245). This involves doing things for the right reasons – i.e. not for profit, approval, reward, fame, admiration or to avoid punishment. All those reasons are extrinsic to the activity itself. And there is something about the means by which we do activities that demonstrate we are focussed on or are appreciating intrinsic or non-instrumental features and values of the activity in question. He notes that things like gardening and cooking have standards which are constitutive of performing them well. And if one cares about the actual activity, not just the outcome or extrinsic benefits of the activity, then they will care about these standards (Peters, 1973: 245).

Peters believed education is central to assist people to learn to adopt this non-instrumental attitude. He claims (1973: 262):

> An educated person ... is characterized not just by his abiding concern for knowledge and understanding but also by the capacity to adopt, to a certain extent, a non-instrumental attitude to activities. How can this attitude be justified? This is not difficult; for the justification of it is implicit in what has already been said. It is presupposed by the determination to search for justification. Anyone who asks the question about his life "Why do this rather than that?" has already reached the stage at which he sees that instrumental justifications must reach a stopping place in activities that must be regarded as providing end-points for such justifications.

In this way, beyond any instrumental benefit or extrinsic value, a person will ultimately seek meaning in what they do. And when such meaning is sought, it is intrinsic to the activity itself: it is brought about by adopting a non-instrumental attitude towards something. And, Peters claims, it is usually directed to the present: the enjoyment of the activity or object in the present moment as contrasted to an instrumental value which is usually forward looking (Peters, 1973: 263). Ultimately, with respect to education, Peters acknowledges the instrumental benefits to individuals and communities in learning, in gaining knowledge and understanding, including (especially) theoretical knowledge. But an educated person, he claims, will do some things for their own sake (Peters, 1973: 266). And in this way, a non-instrumental attitude is adopted, and a non-instrumental benefit gained alongside the instrumental benefits education offers.

Traditionally artists have fought to defend the arts for their own sake, non-instrumentally, rather than for any extrinsic benefit or value the arts may afford. It is engaging with the arts that is often said to be one place such a non-instrumental attitude is best able to be cultivated: in part for some of the reasons Peters offers when referring to education, by which he means theoretical subjects. The arts too are absorbing, interesting, offer you an experience that is designed to have you be entirely present rather than focussed on the past or the future, distracted or bored … At their best, aesthetic experiences are described as time-stopping due to this feeling of being entirely in the moment and caught up in what one is seeing, hearing and noticing in works of art.

It makes sense that multiple experiences may grab one's attention and encourage engagement or perception for the sake of that object and its features alone. Artworks are one excellent source, then, of training the non-instrumental attitude to which Peters refers. This attitude may require exactly the kind of attention (open and receptive) to which I earlier referred as necessary to allow for the emergence of an aesthetic experience when one interacts with or perceives an artwork. By being open and receptive to what is there in front of the viewer, one is perceiving the object in question for its own sake – for what experience it has to offer – and not for the sake of any extrinsic benefit or reward which may be forthcoming at a later date. Thus, the non-instrumental attitude in relation to artworks can be seen to value art for the sake of its aesthetic value – the intrinsic properties of the artwork and the aesthetic experience they afford.

Against instrumentalization

Anti-instrumentalization has deep-roots in philosophical thought. The dominant worry about using things as a means to an end rather than as ends in themselves may be dressed in various cloaks in order to disguise or express the concern at hand. One powerful formation of what is at stake here can be found in one formulation of Immanuel Kant's categorical imperative, which he considers to be the supreme principle of morality. Often called the 'formula of humanity', Kant states, 'so act that you treat humanity, whether in your own person or in the person of any other, always at the same time as an end, never merely as a means' (Kant, 1785: 429). Obviously we sometimes need to use people as a means: for instance, when we are being served by a shop assistant and we are purchasing items, we need them to ring up our order and take payment for goods. But the relevant point is that we shouldn't forget that they are people and not merely cash register machines to be used by us simply for our own convenience.

Kant's deontological approach is often contrasted with utilitarianism, whereby a moral agent focusses on outcomes and maximizing (overall) utility rather than being focussed on duty or the act itself (regardless of consequences). It is evident that there will often exist a tension between doing what is best for the individual versus the overall, greater good: autonomy (I can do whatever I like) versus community (where we compromise or sacrifice for the sake of harmony and to, ideally, maximize everyone's liberty and/or happiness). The worry about adopting a utilitarian approach to (moral) decision making is that sometimes you may indeed need to sacrifice one – or the interests or pleasure of one person – in order to achieve what is best for everyone. Consider, for example, the runaway trolley car dilemma as a classical thought experiment designed to set up these competing intuitions: would you sacrifice one person in order to save five? (D'Olimpio, 2016). When this utilitarian ideal is extended into society, into politics, into economic considerations and into inquiries about the distribution of resources, then the tension may be viewed in terms of the notions of equity versus equality.

Such considerations are relevant in the classroom and in educational policy. Consider, for example, that the attention of a teacher cannot be trained solely on one student in a classroom of thirty, because this is not fair on the other twenty-nine students in the room. This is true even if that one student needs the most help. But a teacher needs to balance the competing interests and demands on her attention in this situation and decide how best to manage the classroom, her students, and her time, effort and energy. Even while she does not view her students as mere means, always as ends in themselves, she must work out how to cover the required content in the allocated time in such a way as to maximize the benefits to classroom learning for all students present in that class. These practical considerations require instrumental or outcomes-based considerations, alongside the deontic questions of duty to individuals.

Many philosophers have raised the concern that people should not be used as things, as objects, for the sake of others, especially in situations in which the ones who are using them as such view themselves as agential (or as Subjects, to use the existentialist term). Historically we have brutal examples of some peoples being used as objects, usually to turn a profit and to benefit others who are more powerful in society. Slavery is one such example. Another way we can read this cause for concern is as a Marxist or socialist response to capitalism and indeed early German Romantics and critical theorists make use of Marxist language to explain their dismay at narrowly utilitarian approaches or policies which reduce all values to one: namely, economic or productive. Naomi Klein argues that the current form of globalization is cloaked in the garb of consumerism, with the efforts of many (usually in developing countries, such as those working in factories) benefitting the interests of those who have *more* – more wealth, power, status, education, opportunities (2014; 2010). Such socio-economic-political critiques ought to be taken seriously as a warning of what to avoid; which is using people as a means to benefit others' ends.

The precise concern is that so much of what we *do* in society – particularly to do with our *work* and ableness; where we put our efforts and energy – is connected to our ability to make money and exert power and influence. Economic values of financial wealth and capital, private property and assets dominate in our world today. Many social justice concerns to do with equality and equity start with a division between those who 'have' and those who do not. But there are more kinds of value than simply economic or use-value; with moral value, hedonistic value and aesthetic value being other obvious types. It seems as though the valuing of objects and money has existed for almost as long as humans have, because we even find Boethius waxing lyrically about the 'pursuit of false goods' in 523 AD in his *The Consolation of Philosophy*. It is Lady Wisdom, Lady Philosophy, who advises he turns away from the pursuit of wealth and status in favour of beatitudo – happiness.

The arts are often proffered as an antidote to the narrowly utilitarian values in life. And this is also true of education when it functions in a certain way – a way that is open and holistic, or student-centred, rather than narrow and dogmatically connected to outcomes (such as test results and fiscal productivity). In this way we can see that the fear and worry about instrumentalizing the arts and education may be connected to the objection about how the totalizing capitalist system over-reaches and dominates in our world today. This political economy extends to see everything in terms of what can be produced, bought, sold or consumed. If everything we do is viewed through such lens, this will shape our justification about what is worthwhile and why, and it even ends up shaping the arts and education in a utilitarian and economic mould to fit one prescribed value type – namely that which is *productive*.

One theorist who connects precisely this type of concern (a worry about the 'neo-liberal agenda') to issues faced in the arts, education and arts education is Gert Biesta. Biesta (2017: 53) explains the problem as being the 'ongoing emphasis on *instrumental justifications* for the role of the arts in education'. He writes:

> The argument about the potential disappearance of art from art education is relatively easy to establish, as this disappearance is visible in the ongoing

emphasis on *instrumental justifications* for the role of the arts in education. Such justifications usually take the form of a statement in which it is claimed that engagement with the arts is *useful* because of its potential significance for or proven impact on 'something else'. In education there is a wide range of options for this 'something else'. This includes the suggestion that engagement with the arts will drive up testable performance in specific curricular domains (most often those that appear to have a high status, such as language, mathematics and science), and it includes the claim that engagement with the arts will promote the development of a range of apparently desirable qualities and skills, such as empathy, morality, creativity, critical thinking, resilience, and so on. Nowadays, claims about the alleged usefulness of the arts are often made 'via' the brain, and sometimes even just plainly in terms of the brain, that is, as the claim that engagement with the arts promotes brain development.

Apart from the fact that Biesta is not convinced such claims can be evidenced, he argues that such instrumental arguments about the benefits of arts education do not really care about art at all. This means art in this context is quite vulnerable, for instance, if something else – another subject – was found to quickly and more effectively and efficiently improve whatever it is for which improvement is being sought, then art would very quickly be discarded in favour of this new method. Or, Biesta notes (2017: 54), 'Art would only remain because it makes schools look "nice" – which, of course, is a public relations argument, not one about art or education.'

Asking the question, 'should art education be useless?', Biesta worries that the only way to counter instrumental justifications for the arts in education is by way of non-instrumental justifications, namely, art for art's own sake. The only viable case is to claim that the arts are useless, devoid of any value beyond art (p. 54). But this is a category mistake, he says, thinking of education in the form of a means for production rather than to look for its meaning. The educated person is not an object, but a person with an altered outlook. So, 'rather than asking what education *produces*, we should be asking what education *means*. And rather than asking what education *makes*, we should be asking what education *makes possible*' (Biesta, 2017: 54).

Extrinsic benefits

While Biesta has a good point to make here about education not being reduced to only be focussed on academic achievement, it is not the case that we can never ask about what education produces. After all, we should consider what are the aims of education, and then, once we have decided upon these, we will want and need ways to test and check to see whether we are meeting these aims. So, if we think education should produce people who know certain things, we do want to test to see whether such knowledge has in fact been learned. But Biesta is an advocate for aimless education – or anti- a pre-determined aim or end goal at least – as for him education is about transformation and the type of transformation that takes place cannot be predicted as it depends entirely on the relationships between the people in a certain context.

For Biesta, the educational gesture, as he calls it, the ambition of education, is about awakening in another the desire to exist in the world in a grown-up way (2017: 85). And art has a central role to play in directing attention to something, to affording observation, which *interrupts* the usual way of looking and encourages people to look, see, and interact with the world. He summarizes this educational ambition of encouraging people to be in dialogue with the world as follows:

> This way of looking at education is obviously not child-centred, but it is also not curriculum-centred, as it is not aimed at getting a curriculum 'inside' the student. Perhaps the best 'label' for it is to call it a 'world-centred' approach, focussing on what it means to exist as subject, in, with and in dialogue with the world, material and social.
>
> (Biesta, 2017: 58)

For Biesta, art may be seen as precisely this: about being in dialogue with the world. The doing of art, he says, 'is precisely this ongoing, literally never-ending exploration of what it might mean to exist in and with the world' (2017: 66).

But on this account, then art is like any other experience that can 'interrupt' and call attention to something. And if it is in the very nature of human beings to interact with the world in which we find ourselves – with others, animals, the environment, objects, etc. – then art may be *good* at commanding our attention or asking us to view things differently or in a new way, but it is not the only thing that does so. And furthermore, it is not clear how this justifies its place on the curriculum. There are many subjects that can encourage a certain kind of perception or attention and interaction. The arts are one amongst many such subjects. What probably matters more on this kind of theory is *how* the subject is taught. Just as art could be taught in a very boring manner, so too could science or history or environmental education be taught in an imaginative and engaged way, encouraging students to *look*, *see*, notice what there is to be noticed and engage with what is being perceived. And such perception surely involves all of the senses; there does not have to be a primacy on the visual (although the metaphor of sight may be more linguistic than analogous for Biesta).

Biesta may be seen to be thinking about the way the arts are taught when he expresses his concern that the arts shouldn't be taught in such a way as to (mostly or solely) emphasize students' subjective expressions of thoughts and feelings. Biesta summarizes that 'art' disappears the more that the arts are instrumentalized in education, and 'education' disappears the more that 'expressivist' approaches to arts education are favoured (2017: 117). The expressivist approach sees the point of arts education as encouraging students' creativity and forms of self-expression. Yet this approach results in increasingly subjective utterances which become devoid of quality or standards because then any creation of art is simply about the individual expressing themselves rather than a focus on the quality of the work or the techniques used or skills employed. Interestingly, as we saw in Chapter 2, such creative self-expression is often one of the stated benefits gained from studying the arts according to many school curricula.

While I am sympathetic to the theorists – like R. S. Peters and Biesta – who warn against instrumentalization and offering instrumental defences for education and arts education, I think there could be a place for supplementing intrinsic defences of the arts and arts education with defences that point out the extrinsic benefits that may be gained from aesthetic education. There are, as Peters conceded, individual and social benefits to education, and this also applies to arts education. However, if a slippery slope starts to occur and defenders of arts education rely increasingly and then dominantly and then solely on instrumental justifications for their subject, then I think we are in trouble. In part because as soon as we use art for the sake of *something else*, we cease to focus on and notice and value the predominant *aesthetic* value that is uniquely and distinctly found in artworks. And then, if *something else* – another subject, perhaps – is able to achieve the extrinsic or instrumental goal *better* – more efficiently or cheaper, say – then there's nothing to prevent that new shiny thing from being brought in to simply replace the arts.

But the main concern is that aesthetic value is simply less valued in our society than other values and in the educational setting this includes academic value (of achievement, merit, quality, and standing) and in wider society this includes economic value. Perhaps this is why artists wish to defend art for art's sake. And this often extends to arts education. Increasingly, however, educators and arts educators in particular are feeling the need to justify what they do in terms of use value, in terms of extrinsic benefits and in terms of how what is being done in the art classroom will increase academic achievement. A recent example of this motivating urge can be seen in extant literature.

In the 2013 OECD publication, *Art for Art's Sake?: The Impact of Arts Education,* the authors provide an overview of empirical research in arts education since 1950 and note that 'research on arts education represents only a tiny share of educational research' (p. 256). They detail three central findings of their literature review. Firstly, there is strong evidence that specific forms of arts education positively impact upon the development of certain skills. For instance, theatre education leads to improved reading and literacy skills. However, theatre is not systematically taught in all classes or schools. Secondly, there is insufficient empirical research done on the correlation between arts education and specific skills such as critical thinking, creativity, motivation and self-identity to be able to make an evidence-based claim that education in the arts positively improves and impacts upon such attributes. However, this is not to deny any impact either, given the relatively small amount of research that has been done on such correlations and how difficult it is to measure these effects. Having said that, arts educators and researchers ought to be nuanced in any assertions they make with respect to the positive outcomes of arts education while also being mindful of poor arts education (which may be due to a variety of factors and highlights important issues such as teacher training, resources and curricula requirements).

The third finding the authors explicate concludes that even if the arts and arts education does not lead to innovation and improved skills that are measurable in quantifiable ways, the arts and arts education nevertheless should occupy an important place within our schools and educational curriculum because art is a human experience. The arts and associated cultural awareness are vital for living the good life, they claim. And this is important. However, it is the final line in the literature review report, and comes on the back of reviewing any empirical research that has been conducted to see what extrinsic benefits may be gleaned from particular arts subjects.

The authors of this literature review note the overall *lack* of empirical research that has been conducted on arts education, particularly when compared to many other types of classroom teaching and learning. They point out that more research is needed if we are to evidence any correlations between arts education and various forms of (especially academic) achievement or extrinsic benefits that may be gleaned from the study and creation of art. It is curious why there is not more empirical research on arts education: is it the lack of funds accessible to those researchers or arts practitioners who might seek to undertake such work? Or a resistance they may have to wanting to investigate arts education in such instrumental terms? Plus the instrumental explanation can seem strange: for example, while it has been evidenced that music students score better in maths and science than their non-musical peers (Guhn, Emerson, & Gouzouasis, 2019), it would be rather odd for people to study music or learn an instrument *in order* to improve their maths or science abilities.

Surely the reason people want to practise the arts – be it playing an instrument or painting or dancing – is because they enjoy or value it and want to master the techniques and skills involved in the activity (even if practising, particularly as a beginner, is not always enjoyable!). This intrinsic justification for the value of the arts may well be supplemented by extrinsic or instrumental justifications. In the case of school-aged children, an obvious example of an extrinsic reason for choosing to study art might be that they are learning to play an instrument because they were encouraged or instructed to do so by their parents or guardians and teachers – the relevant adults in positions of authority in their lives. All the more reason why we need to ensure how we teach the arts to children and young people when they are first exposed to it is enjoyable.

Intrinsic and extrinsic benefits

The desire to defend the arts and arts education in non-instrumental ways is admirable, important, and it makes sense. Given some of the historical and philosophical background which we have very briefly mentioned in this chapter, and the desire for the arts to be appreciated and valued for their own sake and not for the sake of something else that reduces aesthetic value to use value or economic value, there is a lot of resistance towards any instrumentalization of the arts and arts education. And rightly so. In the contemporary context of education more broadly feeling squeezed and moulded to fit a strict set of made-to-measure outcomes, the arts are often seen as an antidote to a narrowly reductive and utilitarian approach by allowing the experience and enjoyment of arts making and reception to be expansive and valued for its own sake: for the aesthetic experiences the arts afford.

I obviously agree to some extent with the concern about instrumentalizing arts education given that the defence I mount of compulsory aesthetic education is justified in non-instrumental terms, in terms of the intrinsic benefits to be gained from arts making and reception. And while I do not wish to see the value of the arts or arts education reduced to instrumental value/s and/or extrinsic benefits, I also think it does not necessarily harm education in the arts to point out and endorse some instrumental values that accompany the arts and aesthetic education. Among these may be insights into history, ideology and other learning that comes from engaging with great artworks. For instance, as Nathan Ross (2017: 1) notes, 'aesthetic experience is not merely a passive response to art: it is an indispensable way to gain critical insight into the social and political context of our lives'. I would like there to be room for extrinsic benefits and values of arts education to be expressed and recognized, even if the value that should be first and foremost acknowledged and celebrated is an intrinsic or aesthetic one.

One of the reasons I think it is important to allow for and happily praise and endorse the arts based on some extrinsic benefits and values is when doing so removes some of the barriers people, especially young people, face when exploring their options and desires to study and create art, and due to their enjoyment of the arts wish to seek employment in the creative arts industries. For example, one worry many people may have is that the arts will not lead to a successful career, where 'successful' implies remuneration and financial benefits. This is the stereotypical response we see (often depicted in the arts themselves including many narrative artworks) whereby parents worry their children will not be able to make a living by working in the arts as a struggling musician or painter or actor or writer. The parental response when their children tell them they want to focus on arts subjects, particularly if they are more interested in the arts than they are in other academic subjects, can cause a barrier and create tension and difficulties between the child and parents or guardians and teachers.

The 'responsible adult' in that young person's life may feel the need to steer them towards academic subjects which they believe may be more likely to result in sensible and successful (there's that word again) career options. So there is much to be said for educating children about the financial benefits that may accompany careers in the arts industries.

The creative arts contribute a significant sum to countries' gross domestic income in developed Western countries – for instance, in the United States:

> The entire U.S. arts and culture sector (i.e., nonprofit, commercial, education) is a $764 billion industry. This represents 4.2 percent of the nation's Gross Domestic Product (GDP) – a larger share of the economy than transportation, agriculture, or construction – according to the U.S. Bureau of Economic Analysis.
>
> (Cohen, 2019)

In Australia, the creative economy employs more people than the mining and agriculture sectors combined and contributes to gross national value as much as the employment and training sector and almost twice that of the agriculture, forestry and fishing sector. In fact,

> the most recent accounting from the Australian Bureau of Statistics reports cultural and creative activity plays an important role in Australia's economy, growing to $115.8 billion in 2018–19, a 27.4 per cent increase over the last 10 years, and contributing a six per cent share of GDP.
>
> (Cunningham, 2022)

And in the UK,

> our Creative Industries have been growing faster than twice the rate of the wider UK economy since 2010. In 2019, they were worth more than life sciences, automotive, aerospace, and oil and gas combined. In 2020, exports of creative services were worth £41.4 billion, while exports of creative goods stood at £8.9 billion. In 2021, our industry employed 2.3 million people, a 49% increase since 2011.
>
> (Creative Industries Trade and Investment Board, 2022: 4)

Meanwhile in Aotearoa New Zealand,

> a new report shows that books, music, television and film sectors of New Zealand's creative industries annually contribute more than $3.5 billion to the local economy.
>
> By comparison, these components of the creative industries are similar in size to the forestry sector, double the size of the printing sector, and half the size of sheep, beef cattle and grain farming.
>
> (WeCreate, 2018)

The arts were some of the hardest hit industries during the global pandemic with significant economic losses from 2019 to 2021, which have effected the global economy while leaving individual artists out of work. Data from the United Nations estimates that between 2019 and 2020 there was a $750 billion contraction in gross value that is usually added by the creative economy (the arts and creative industries) globally due to the effects of the pandemic (National Endowment for the Arts, 2021; The Policy Circle, 2022).

Writing in relation to Australia, but with his comments applicable to other developed Western countries, Stuart Cunningham (2022) proclaims that

> the role of creative skills in the evolution of our future economy needs to become mainstream knowledge. Creative skills are some of the least likely to be supplanted by automation and they have been integral to fast-growing industries over the last decade. Of the top five most innovation-active industries, between 10 and 28 per cent of employees hold a creative qualification.

All of this is to say that there are jobs in the creative arts industries and if someone loves the arts and wants to work in the creative arts, we shouldn't allow extrinsic reasons to be a barrier that prevents them from even trying to pursue their dream in the first instance. As we want to see these young people grow up to be able to lead flourishing and meaningful lives, they may well desire a lifestyle in which they earn an income based on some artistic or creative pursuit that they really enjoy, are talented at and will find rewarding. The statistics above demonstrate that the clichéd parental refrain 'oh, but there's no money in that … you won't be able to earn a living as an artist' is not true, and should not provide sufficient reason to prevent talented creative types from pursuing the arts if they are enjoying their studies in the arts.

Conclusion

While acknowledging that arts education should be defended in non-instrumental ways, I nevertheless acknowledge the importance of any instrumental benefits that are associated with arts education and the role of the arts within society. As has already been acknowledged in Chapters 2 and 3, the arts may do many things, including supporting self-expression and moral formation through the cultivation of a sympathetic attitude. There are multiple ways that the arts are understood to contribute to individuals and to society, some of which are instrumentally beneficial.

As we saw in Chapter 3, one concern being rendered visible was that ascribing cognitive outcomes to aesthetic education in order to defend its seat at the scholarly table may also work against the arts as subjects that resist the narrow place set at the academic table. Many advocates for the arts express the importance of not reducing the value of the arts to instrumental and measurable gains. It must be noted that Elliot Eisner argues that the cognitive benefits gained form an intrinsic aspect of engagement with the arts. I do not deny that there are some measurable cognitive benefits gained from engagement with the arts and an arts-based educational curriculum. However, the worry may be that the arts are justified or used *for* their cognitive benefits, rather than the cognitive benefits emerging from a valuing of the arts and aesthetic education.

Throughout this book, I have justified and critiqued philosophical arguments that seek to defend the unique and essential contribution the arts make in terms of their creation and reception, as a form of self-expression, imaginative engagement, cognitive as well as affective experience, source of individual and social reflection and contemplation, all of which also confer instrumental benefits upon individuals and society. While the reason I defend aesthetic education is based on an essentialist and non-instrumental defence of the role for aesthetic experience in the flourishing life, there are supplementary roles for the arts and for arts education that do not diminish my primary argument.

In practical terms, sometimes an instrumental argument may need to be mounted to respond to a nay-sayer: for example the parent who doesn't want their child to focus on the arts at the expense of their academic studies due to their idea that this will be unlikely to result in good (successful) career opportunities after mandatory schooling has been completed. An economic and financial argument is certainly not the reason I would give as a justification for teaching the arts in schools, but as a defence for the student who wants to pursue the arts and needs to reply to their parents who prioritize economic value over aesthetic value, then yes, by all means, be informed and explain the economic value of the creative industries alongside the benefits to a fulfilled and meaningful, autonomous life.

However, I must admit that it is vital that arts teachers do not sacrifice all essentialist defences of the arts and arts education in the face of any pressure felt from educational policymakers who might prefer the arts to be justified on the curriculum due to their role in relation to other academic achievements such as numeracy and literacy. As has been explored throughout this chapter, any pressure on educational goals to be increasingly narrowly academic and achievement-oriented is a cause for concern. Education and schooling should be broader than simply STEM-focussed, or include more than the goals of literacy and numeracy. Ideally it is whole-child focussed, and the arts are ideally suited to be holistic in this way. As Laura-Lee Kearns (2015: 115) notes:

> Any pedagogy that chooses to recognize the whole person would have to include the arts as integral to the curriculum. One's active participation in the arts, whether it be making, viewing, analyzing, discussing, or wonder-ing, brings us closer to living harmoniously with ourselves and others.

The arts do not stand in isolation from other values and facets of life. We are human beings, making and receiving artworks – or teaching the arts – in a context, so of course there are political, ethical and financial considerations that come to bear upon what we can do and how. In the next chapter I will be critically engaging with the moral value and ethical messages that may be found in artworks, with a particular focus on how the arts teacher might engage students in dialogue about these. Such debates reveal the interesting and vexing tensions between aesthetics and ethics that ought to be reflected upon and carefully considered. Such tensions can also be meaningfully explored in relation to the curriculum. For example, the question of which art examples we should use in the classroom is important and has ethical and political impact, particularly given the recent focus on decolonizing the curriculum and expanding the canon. In these ways, the aesthetic, political, economic, moral and social values are identified as influencing the arts and arts education, and the interplay and overlap between these values with respect to the same ought to be considered.

7

Aesthetics and ethics

Introduction

Amongst the debates that have raged within the field of philosophical aesthetics is whether or not the ethical value of an artwork may be taken into consideration when judging the overall aesthetic value of that artwork. The choice of position taken effects what one can say about the ethical value of an artwork, how it is to be evaluated and, further, its implications for society (for instance, in terms of censorship). The two main aesthetic positions that oppose each other are those of the aestheticist (also known as autonomism) and the moralist between which lies a graduated scale that allows for greater or less compromise. These include the positions of moderate autonomism, moderate moralism and ethicism.[1]

To simplify the positions, the ethicist (moderate moralism and ethicism) answers *yes*, there is a moral value of artworks that affects its overall aesthetic value, while the aesthete (the autonomist) states *no*. For the aesthete, even if there is a moral value of an artwork, this will not (or should not) affect the work of art's overall value as the overall value of a work of art should be based solely upon its aesthetic value.[2] Richard Posner (1997; 1998) backs artists such as W. H. Auden, George Orwell and Oscar Wilde who famously wrote, 'There is no such thing as a moral or an immoral book. Books are well written, or badly written. That is all' (Wilde, 1891: preface).

Against the aesthetes, on the other side of the debate, are proponents of ethical criticism such as Martha Nussbaum (1990; 1998a), Wayne C. Booth (1988; 1998), Noël Carroll (1996; 1998b) and Mary Devereaux (1998; 2004). While much has been written about the ethical criticism of narrative artworks, not enough attention has been paid to the educational implications of this debate.

While the appeal of aestheticism is to protect the creative expression of artists and their works, this poses an educational challenge for teachers who wish their students to be critically engaged viewers. In so far as an artwork contains a moral and/or political message, the viewer of the work ought to critically engage with it, and sometimes this is unavoidable. For instance, if there is a beautiful artwork to which I have a strong – either positive or negative – moral response, as a viewer I would find this very difficult to set aside and just appreciate the beauty of the work in question. There are many examples of precisely this – particularly when the aesthetic value and the moral value of the artwork are in tension. Well-known examples include Mark Twain's *Huckleberry Finn* and Vladimir Nabokov's *Lolita*.

Therefore, the ethical content and/or context of an artwork may interfere with or impact upon my ability to receive an aesthetic experience from it, or an ethical judgement may usurp the artist's intended aesthetic meaning. This feature of artworks, whereby the aesthetic and ethical values may clash, is relevant to aesthetic education and therefore art teachers must consider how they will deal with such instances. This is particularly true today in an era of cancel culture whereby the question will be asked about what should or should not be shown, displayed, or taught.

In this chapter, I will critically detail the positions of aestheticism and ethicism and consider the educational implications of each. I ultimately defend the view that the value ascribed to a work may be a (positive or negative) moral value, and this moral value may affect the overall aesthetic value of the work of art. This needn't result in censorship but should allow for critical engagement with art.

Approaching the issue of aesthetics and ethics from an educational point of view, I believe it is undeniable to grant that artworks are powerful vehicles for moral sentiments and meaning, and they offer experiences to people that they might not otherwise encounter. Therefore it is important that viewers are taught to engage critically with art in terms of both aesthetics and ethics. While these values may occasionally clash (in fact, the most interesting examples are precisely when this conflict occurs within one work of art and/or its reception), we must find a way forward, as viewers as well as educationally.

Aestheticism

Autonomism, also known as 'aestheticism', states that art and ethics are autonomous realms of value. Autonomists argue that the only relevant evaluation of an artwork is that of the aesthetic as it is only an artistic focus that is relevant *qua* work of art. Radical autonomism, such as the position held by Clive Bell (1914) from the Bloomsbury Group, states that it doesn't even make sense to assess a work of art in terms of morality (or politics or cognition) (Young, 2005: 70). Aesthetes such as Bell claim that an artwork should be evaluated only in terms of its formal aspects; namely the aesthetic qualities which may include form, expression, unity, composition, line, colour, shape, tone, texture and pattern. Unfortunately, agreement is lacking regarding those features that are considered to be both necessary and sufficient in supporting an evaluation of the artwork and its ensuing aesthetic experience. The aesthete defines aesthetic experience as, 'the experience prescribed by an artwork that is valued for its own sake (and not for the sake of anything else, including moral enlightenment or moral improvement)' (Carroll, 2000: 353). In this way, the position of the radical autonomist has evolved as a theoretical argument whereby the very definition of aesthetic evaluation is based on what is categorically or conceptually unique to all artworks, which entails the exclusion of moral evaluation. The position known as moderate autonomism allows for a moral assessment to be made of an artwork yet argues that the work's moral value does not affect the aesthetic value, which is the overall value of the artwork.

Autonomists try to protect 'high art' from censure and from being reduced to everyday values such as commercialism by arguing that the ethical realm has nothing to do with that of the aesthetic. In fact, we can think of examples of moralizing in artworks that reduce the artistic value or appreciation of the work due to the heavy-handed moral message seeking to grab the spectator's attention where the artwork may feel like a vehicle for the values presented. For instance, Aesop's fables are one such example, whose purpose was primarily moral education. For aesthetes, it is the aesthetic experience that should be primary, not secondary, when encountering an artwork, and experience of the aesthetic good is conceptually distinct from moral goodness.

Furthermore, aestheticists claim that the aesthetic experience, defined in terms of disinterested attention and independent of ethics, is the common denominator applicable to all art and should therefore be the standard of judgement for all artworks. In defence of this 'common-denominator' argument, the autonomist explains that the formal features of a work of art when appropriately (aesthetically) engaged with produce an aesthetic experience which *is* the aesthetic value and thus the overall value of a work of art (Carroll, 2000: 352). Thus, for an art object to be valued as art it must be capable of eliciting from the viewer an aesthetic experience.

Educational implications of aestheticism

The ethicist/aestheticist debate is relevant in terms of its influence upon the critical evaluation of artworks that affects our recognition and evaluation of the impact of art. It is also educationally important because arts educators are teaching students *how* to engage with artworks: how to value them and how to receive them. If we consider that the aesthete is primarily and often exclusively concerned with the aesthetic features of, experience of, and value of artworks, we can see that for art educators this justifies a protected space in which students can engage with art in a liberal manner.

Aestheticism protects the place for art in society, and for artists' free, creative expression. It is anti-censorship and given that censorship of art often hinges on the moral and political messages of artworks and the role such art may play in influencing citizens (particularly young people), aestheticism protects art and creative expression from such moral and political judgements. In this same way aestheticism also separates art from its (wider) educational impact because it is concerned with art for its own sake and not for the sake of its impact (educational or otherwise).

Aestheticist Posner declares that 'immersion in literature does not make us better citizens or better people' (1997: 2). Yet there is a growing interest in research in character education as to whether good literature and poetry can indeed make us better people (see Booth, 1988; Bohlin, 2005; Carr, 2005; Carr and Harrison, 2015; D'Olimpio, Paris and Thompson, 2022). It is understandable why art lovers wish to defend the value of art for its own sake. And yet, artists and artworks play a significant role in encouraging reflection upon human activity. The place of art and the role for artists in society can be contentious precisely due to the moral, social and political impact of art – a fact of which aesthetes are well aware. Certainly Posner does not deny it, concluding his article by stating, 'The formal properties do not exhaust the worth and appeal of literature, but the moral properties, I suggest, are almost sheer distraction' (1997: 24). This suggests that arts educators are better off focussing on the aesthetic qualities of a work of art rather than the ethical features on the aestheticist position.

One educational role for art includes highlighting society's ethical, social and political actions. Thus it seems odd, and counter-intuitive, to insist we cannot speak about art in ethical terms, particularly when art is sometimes used to promote or critique certain moral, political and social messages. Against the aestheticist, where artworks prescribe an audience response that invokes morality and ethics, surely the moral value of the work in question is a component of the overall aesthetic experience. Some of the pleasure and absorption we feel when engaging with artworks or when overwhelmed by them is ethical; our reception and experience of some artworks will necessarily involve moral condemnation, ethical celebration, consideration of virtuous and vicious character traits, etc.

Such a claim is most obvious in examples of narrative artworks such as novels, plays and films. For example, famous aesthete Oscar Wilde is known for arguing, in the preface of *The Picture of Dorian Gray* (1891), that there is no such thing as a good or bad book, rather, books are well or badly written and that is all. Yet Wilde's books contain moral messages that are almost impossible for the reader to ignore and he took the line of the aesthete in order to publish such sentiments and avoid censorship or rebuke (unsuccessfully in his case). When Wilde defended aestheticism he was doing so precisely because he knew he would be accused of impacting upon people via his art (Freedman, 1993: 51–2). Wilde's own interest in the debate was not in reference to the aesthetic/moral issue at hand, but rather the impact that people were trying to say his art had, and the impact he wished it to have. It is widely acknowledged that his art *did* have, and continues to have, a lasting moral impact.

We learn from narrative artworks. And Wilde's texts are completely concerned with the ethical in such a way that sees the values of art and morality as both present in the one text. It is the moral message of *Dorian Gray* that largely contributed to making it a great work; it is the moral value of the work that enhances its overall, aesthetic value. This may be because, in this instance, the moral message is an intrinsic part of the work, a formal feature of the narrative artwork, and in this way will necessarily count towards its overall value.

Allowing for the ethical evaluation of artworks need not result in censorship of artists and their work. However, where we find a moral message in an artwork, and given that art affects us emotionally as well as cognitively, artworks must be subject to ethical evaluation as well as aesthetic evaluation. As Booth argues against Posner, 'As every reader of Wilde knows, whenever we fully engage with any story, we engage not with abstract concepts or moral codes but with *persons,* both with the characters in the story and the implied person who has chosen to portray them in this precise way' (Booth, 1998: 375, italics in the original). And, as educators, we want to teach students to engage critically, compassionately and creatively with the artworks they encounter; with fictional characters and scenarios, with the overall messages and meanings gleaned from texts as well as with their authors. If this is true, then we cannot rely upon aestheticism; we must instead move to a position that allows for ethical criticism of artworks.

Ethicism

Two positions that accommodate the fact that artworks are created in, and impact upon the world ethically are moderate moralism as advocated by Noël Carroll (1996; 1998a; 1998b; 2000) and Berys Gaut's ethicism (1998). Moderate moralism holds that some works are concerned with morality and in such cases moral evaluation is relevant and may impact upon the work's overall aesthetic value. However, works that aren't concerned with morality, and lack ethical content and implications, are not appropriate objects of ethical criticism. Carroll notes that 'even if there were a single criterion of value for all art, that would not have to preclude the possibility that there are not also multiple, local criteria of evaluation for certain genres of art, consistent with whatever the global criterion turns out to be' (Carroll, 2000: 358).

For example, an artwork that has a moral message has a relevant ethical value that may or may not impact upon the aesthetic value of the work. The aesthetic value therefore is not determined by this ethical value alone – it can also, or even predominantly be determined by aesthetic features of the work. Ethicism is similar to the position of the moderate moralist, yet the ethicist takes a slightly stronger line when arguing for the ethical impact of an artwork upon the overall value of that work. Ethicism claims that ethical value is *always* relevant to aesthetic value if it is included in an artwork.

The autonomist claims that in society it is *only* artworks that are *primarily* intended to promote aesthetic experience and thus they should be evaluated solely in terms of that to which they uniquely aim. Yet artworks that combine aesthetic experience with social, moral and/or political messages are by no means uncommon. Examples range from the earliest religious art to any number of popular songs by artists concerned with social, political, environmental and economic issues that impact ethically upon society. The position of aestheticism doesn't do justice to these kinds of artworks, whose aesthetic experience includes understanding the relevant ethical messages imbued in the work. As Devereaux points out, Posner takes the ethical messages in works of literature to be optional extras, to which one may choose to attend to or not and, 'like most aestheticists, Posner recommends the latter' (2004: 8). Yet as Devereaux argues, 'some kinds of moral judgements ... take the literary work itself as their object' (2004: 8). This means that the ethical judgement, in order to be appropriately made, requires aesthetic sensibility.

Narrative artworks can be subtle and complex. In order to judge them accurately, one needs to attend to them properly, aesthetically, in order to glean an appropriate reading of the work as well as the prescribed aesthetic experience. However, as will be discussed in further detail in the next section, it is also the case that some aesthetic features of the artwork require appropriate ethical responses in order to respond properly to the artwork *qua* artwork.

The position of the ethicist, who defends either moderate moralism or ethicism, is more plausible as a theory of how we evaluate artworks and how we should evaluate the aesthetic experience and overall aesthetic value of art. This is because the moral message of an artwork may impact upon (support or negate, interrupt or augment) the aesthetic experience one has when engaging with an artwork that contains ethical components. Importantly, it is these components that are being evaluated as an aspect of the artwork in question and, therefore, it is also these components educators want their students to learn how to engage with, in both an open, receptive manner and a critically engaged manner. I will give an example of why I think this is important and persuasive, by considering when the ethical flaw is also, one and the same time, a formal flaw in the artwork.

Moral flaws as aesthetic flaws

As mentioned earlier, the (moderate) autonomist may compromise slightly and allow for an ethical reading of an artwork that contains an ethical component, provided the ethical value does not in any way affect the aesthetic value and vice versa. This is a position that maintains that the ethical and aesthetical spheres of value are autonomous. However, ethical critics may argue that an ethical blemish in an artwork affects the artwork as a whole and thus impacts upon its aesthetic value as well. Taking ethicism as our working example, when we take an 'all-things-considered' view of the work *qua* artwork, certain ethical failings in an artwork are *always* going to be aesthetic defects and, in this way, formal flaws in the work (Carroll, 2000: 375). Thus, as aesthetic defects, these ethical defects may affect the overall value of the art object.

The classic example ethical critics often give is Leni Riefenstahl's *Triumph of the Will*, an infamous propaganda film covering a Nazi party rally held in Nuremberg, Germany in 1934. Beautifully shot with stunning cinematography, the aesthetic value of the film is undermined by its portrayal of Hitler as a moral political leader who simply wanted the best for all Germans. It is a piece of propaganda disguised as a documentary and the moral message of the film interrupts the aesthetic appreciation of the artwork (Devereaux, 1998). The ethicist claims that, in this example, it can be seen how the ethical defect of the work (negatively) affects its overall aesthetic evaluation. Ethicism also allows for the ethical message of a work to positively affect its overall aesthetic evaluation.

Arguing that moral flaws can be defects in an artwork, the ethicist offers the 'merited response argument' where prescribed responses to artworks are either merited or unmerited by the narrative. If an artwork portrays an immoral message while prescribing aesthetic engagement, the immoral message may be unmerited and constitute an aesthetic defect in the work *qua* artwork if it interferes with the aesthetic engagement and prescribed uptake of the work in question (Carroll, 2000: 375). For instance, there may be an unsympathetic character to whom the reader is invited to adopt a non-satirical, sincerely sympathetic attitude towards. Yet if the reader simply cannot do so due to the manner in which the character has been portrayed, then this is a flaw in the novel, not in the reader response. In this way, immoral responses to artworks, 'notably prescribing immoral cognitive-affective responses', the ethicist argues, are unmerited and give the audience reason to refrain from responding in the way that the artwork dictates (Carroll, 2000: 375).

Thus, contrary to moderate autonomism and autonomism, moral defects in a work of art *may* be aesthetic flaws in the work. Uptake (or lack thereof) results from an audience member's (in)ability to engage appropriately with the artwork in question and thus supports the ethicist's position that moral defects in a work of art may impact upon its overall (aesthetic) value. It does this by interfering with, blocking or altering the kind of aesthetic experience we are able to glean from the artwork in question.

The reason this matters in an educational sense is because of how we teach young people to engage with artworks. We may consider that, in arts education, we are aiming to educate students to be appropriately sensitive audience members: well positioned to make the most appropriate (charitable as well as suitably critical) readings of works of art. If we were to adopt the position of aestheticism, we would only focus on teaching students to appreciate the skill with which the words/paint/images are used, the style of the writing, the expression of the characters/dancers and the beauty of the artwork/performance piece. We would be encouraging an aesthetic experience based on those formal features (form, expression, unity, composition, line, colour, shape, tone, texture and pattern) but may discourage a moral or political reading of a work or expressly teach the student that the moral or political meaning or value of the work does not affect or impact upon its overall *aesthetic* value.

This is fine when the artwork in question contains no ethical or political message, of which there may be some. However, there are many artworks, especially narrative artworks, that simply cannot avoid the fact that they are imbued with ethical and political meaning. Understanding and engaging appropriately with such works necessarily involve understanding these ethical and political aspects to the work. If you do not understand them, you are unlikely to be fully appreciating the work and experiencing what is there for you to experience as a result of engaging appropriately with the work. Nussbaum (1998a: 358) contends:

> One can think of works of art which can be contemplated reasonably well without asking any urgent questions about how one should live. Abstract formalist paintings are sometimes of this character, and some intricate but non-programmatic works of music (though by no means all). But it seems highly unlikely that a responsive reading of any complex literary work is utterly detached from concerns about time and death, about pain and the transcendence of pain, and so on – all the material of 'how one should live' questions as I have conceived it.

While some artworks may not require one to bring to bear any ethical or political values when engaging with it, this is not the case when it comes to *all* artworks and certainly is not the case in relation to narrative artworks.

With narrative artworks, such as works of literature, plays and films, there is always going to be some social, political and ethical messages in the work that are going to be important to understand if one is to understand the work in question. But, further, as educators, we want such messages to be engaged with not just in an open and receptive manner, but in a critically engaged manner as well. According to Murdoch, judgements about values are unavoidable in narrative works as, 'one cannot avoid value judgements. Values show, and show clearly, in literature' (quoted in Magee, 1978: 278). Value judgements are embedded in our language and the words we use often imply or presume certain kinds of moral evaluations. Murdoch (1998: 27–8) notes:

> It is important to remember that language itself is a moral medium, almost all uses of language convey value. This is one reason why we are almost always morally active. Life is soaked in the moral, literature is soaked in the moral ... So the novelist is revealing his values by any sort of writing which he may do. He is particularly bound to make moral judgements in so far as his subject-matter is the behaviour of human beings.

And so, to the extent that artworks contain moral and political meaning, teaching our students to critically and compassionately engage with these stories, characters and the situations in which they find themselves is not only a part of understanding and appreciating the work in question, and constitutive of the associated aesthetic experience where it is present in the artwork, but it is important pedagogically as well.

Murdoch and Nussbaum refer to the positive effects of engaging with *good* (aesthetically and ethically) literature, and they are optimistic about the role for literature and narrative artworks in educational spaces. As Nussbaum remarks, the arts and the humanities work to activate and expand our capacity 'to see the world through another person's eyes' (2010: 96). Yet there are also examples in which educators should teach students to engage critically with the ethical messages contained in artworks because they may not be so positive or virtuous. And this is even more important when the aesthetic quality of the work is very good, beautiful or engaging.

Returning to the example of *Triumph of the Will*, which is often cited as being aesthetically good despite its immoral message: if the viewer, especially the young viewer, isn't critically engaged with the moral and political messages of the film, then they are simply swept up in the beauty, magnificence, power and exuberance of Hitler and Nazi Germany. This would be worrying to educators precisely because of the (im)moral messages conveyed through Nazism. On the other hand, if our viewer is critically engaged with the film, they may find it difficult to purely enjoy the film and have a full aesthetic experience as a result, precisely due to the (im)moral element of the work. The latter can be explained perfectly on the position of moderate moralism or ethicism because we can see that the prescribed audience response, to love and celebrate Hitler and Nazi Germany, is *ethically* unwarranted, and, in the case of this propaganda documentary, therefore also an aesthetic or formal flaw. The ethical failing of the work interrupts and interferes with one's aesthetic uptake of the work precisely because it is unavoidable in the meaning. The appropriately sensitive audience member cannot, in this case, divorce the ethical judgement from the work and, I claim, neither would we want them to or think that they should.

Engaging with the work means engaging with all of these elements and, as educators, we should teach students this. Devereaux (1998: 354) notes that if we bracket the political message of certain works of art, such as Orwell's *1984*, and solely appreciate the formal features of the work, or admire *Triumph of the Will* purely for its beauty, then we miss an essential element of the work. This claim and examples such as these challenge the position known as aestheticism which insists on keeping the realms of aesthetics and ethics separate in relation to works of art.

Aesthetic and moral education

As we have seen, I allow some moral features of artworks to count as formal features in the artworks that possess them, and therefore, an element of the aesthetic experience in such instances may indeed be ethical or informed by ethical judgements. This allows for some aspect of the intrinsic value of some artworks to have an ethical component; particularly in the case of narrative artworks, but only when that ethical component is a part of the overall aesthetical value of the work, as allowed for on ethicism or moderate moralism. This, however, differs from using the arts for the purpose of moral learning or for the cultivation of virtuous character traits, as was discussed in Chapter 2. As I have already made clear, I am not against careful use of the arts to support moral education, but I do see such use as instrumental, whereby the arts are being taught for the sake of (potential) extrinsic benefits. This moral education may be a supplementary argument for teaching the arts, but should not be the primary justification for aesthetic education.

History reminds us that certain texts and artworks were deemed virtuous and praised, commissioned and displayed while others were censored and destroyed by the authorities in positions of power who sought to convey and perpetuate certain ideas and values. This kind of censorship is something to which the aesthete strongly objects and, as educators, this should also be something we consider, when selecting artworks for inclusion on the arts curriculum. The question of *which* artworks and *which* or *whose* morals are allowed to be influential is inescapable here, and this inevitably highlights the concern to do with whose voices are neglected or omitted.

Given we are aware of how narrow the traditional view is about what should count as great art, the art teacher has the chance to widen the canon for the sake of the students who are learning about art. There are some really interesting artworks done which reflect upon the narrowness of the traditional canon and seek to expand it. For example, consider work by the Guerrilla Girls, such as their piece entitled 'Guerrilla Girls' Pop Quiz' (1990), displayed at the Tate Modern in London, UK. The funky poster-style visual artwork asks, 'Q. If February is Black History Month and March is Women's History Month, what happens the rest of the year?' The answer, 'A. discrimination', is printed in bold, upside down like this is a playing card from a game of trivia. Another artwork, a poster by the Guerrilla Girls on display at London's Saatchi gallery (2023), asks, 'Are there more naked women than women artists in art museums? Visit your favourite museum, count 'em up, & let the Guerrilla Girls know!' This would make a fun and informative activity for a class visit to a museum or art gallery and the art teacher could facilitate an important dialogue on this theme afterwards.

Along with themed curated exhibitions, many art galleries now offer resources to support this more inclusive attitude towards art, resources that may be used by the art teacher in the classroom. For instance, the Tate galleries have an online guide entitled 'Women and Power' on their website (https://www.tate.org.uk/art/women-art-tate/women-and-power) that encourages visitors to the site to 'Explore stories of women's empowerment across the centuries through works in our collection'. There are also groups such as the Feminist Art Coalition (FAC, https://feministartcoalition.org/), based in the United States of America, who see art as a 'catalyst for discourse and civic engagement'. On their website, guided by their motto 'Engage. Reflect. Act.', they explain:

> The Feminist Art Coalition (FAC) is a platform for art projects informed by feminisms*. FAC fosters collaboration between arts institutions that aim to make public their commitment to social justice and structural change. It seeks to generate cultural awareness of feminist thought, experience, and action.

The explicit linking between the aesthetic, the political, the social and the ethical in these multimedia platforms is clearly designed to be educational and is worth engaging with. Furthermore, they offer young people the chance to think, critique, reflect and then look forward – with a view to challenging past assumptions, considering what has changed, and muse, imagine and strategize as to what needs to happen next.

Just because we can make moral judgements of artworks does not mean we should censor or restrict their creation and reception – and arguably this applies to historical artworks as well, even as our social mores update. However, it is understandable that the aesthete may be worried about the consequences of the moral judgements passed on artworks. Given that the ethicist claims that a work of art can be judged morally, and this impacts upon the overall value of an artwork, they may then go on (quite easily) to argue that *bad* moral artworks can have a negative impact upon its viewers and perhaps even society as a whole. And perhaps this is of real concern to the ethicist – that the moral messages in artworks *will* influence the viewers and audiences of these works; it may *harm* members of our society and the community or simply change existing social norms. Aestheticists may welcome the fact that art can effect change, but ultimately they wish to protect artists and their artworks. Ultimately it recognized that art is powerful.

Yet, for educators, this is also why we should educate students to engage respectfully, critically and sympathetically with artworks. We need not deny that art can be influential, may present various perspectives and offer new ways of thinking about things. But from this it need not follow that such free, creative expression be suppressed, repressed, censored or banned, even if there will always be exceptional cases to consider. What does follow, educationally, is the need to teach students to be critically engaged viewers who are still able to appreciate and value art for its aesthetic experience.

The aesthete holds that while a moral value may be given to an artwork, this has nothing to do with that work's aesthetic and therefore overall value. On this view, an art object may be morally 'bad' yet aesthetically 'good' and therefore its overall value as an artwork can be deemed good. This overall value must therefore be seen to be disconnected from how an artwork is used or how its impact upon society is judged. For instance, if the artwork is used in an ethically deplorable manner and this use has a negative impact upon society, this is, on the aesthete's argument, a case of a good artwork being used in a bad way.

Using the example of *Triumph of the Will*, the aesthete can maintain that the work of art is beautiful (if they do think it beautiful), aesthetically pleasing and the overall artistic value of the work is high, despite its negative moral message. The aesthete may claim that *the use* of this film is morally and ethically wrong; it was used as a piece of Nazi propaganda, and this is clearly immoral. Yet, the aesthete argues that the work in and of itself is fine, despite its moral component and its use being morally deplorable. The question that ethicists ask the aesthete is, how can the intrinsic moral meaning of the work be denied formal attribution to the piece? Further difficult questions follow. Is the artist responsible for this artwork that was intentionally made with a flawed moral message? This question is particularly interesting when one considers that a work may be used in a way other than that intended by its author. And appropriate display and exhibition is another important consideration that has also been the subject of debate with respect to works by Riefenstahl, Wagner, Donald Friend and others.[3]

The complex, difficult and nuanced nature of such debates to do with aesthetics and ethics, potential limits to free, creative expression and appropriate audiences/display of contentious artworks are those that benefit from educational facilitation. Carroll (2000: 378) notes, 'Artworks can be immensely subtle in terms of their moral commitments. Morally defective portrayals may elude even morally sensitive audiences and may require careful interpretation in order to be unearthed.' Thus, encouraging students to think about and explore such ideas in educational spaces such as the art class is an important part of teaching young people to become appropriately sensitive audience members. Such audience members are sympathetic to artworks, open to receiving the aesthetic experience available to them by engaging with the artwork in question, yet they are also critically active, particularly because art affects our emotions as well as our cognition. Where and when artworks contain moral, social and political messages, appropriately sensitive audience members will engage with those too. In this way, ethicism is the most appropriate position for arts educators to adopt.

Conclusion

In this chapter I have detailed the position known as aestheticism (autonomism and moderate autonomism) and compared this to the position defended by the ethicist (moderate moralism and ethicism). The aesthete claims that even if there is a moral value of an artwork, this will not (or should not) affect the work of art's overall value as the overall value of a work of art should be based solely upon its aesthetic value. However, the ethicist, adopting an all-things-considered perspective, argues that the moral value of artworks can be gleaned, judged, and may affect the overall value of a work of art. I have defended the ethicist, offering examples of when ethical failings in a work may also be aesthetic flaws which can interfere with the prescribed audience response and any aesthetic experience the viewer may potentially have by engaging with the work in question. But, most importantly, I have viewed this debate in aesthetics through an educational lens and considered the educational implications of aestheticism and ethicism.

It is vitally important that students are taught to value the aesthetic and formal features of artworks and appreciate aesthetic experience. I see it as central to arts education that students are also taught to value the creative expression of artists and their works, even as these often push social boundaries and offer new and sometimes challenging perspectives. However, while this open, receptive and creative approach to art is at the heart of arts education, this doesn't necessitate switching off one's critical engagement, which includes critically engaging with the ethical and political messages gleaned from art. Where we find artworks containing moral and/or political messages, the viewer of the work ought to critically engage with these. This is the case to ensure they understand and appreciate the work (which may include considering contextual elements in relation to when the work was made) and also so they are not at risk of being uncritical in relation to the messages conveyed through art media.

It may be that the art teacher may bypass any moral risk by carefully selecting which artworks the students engage with, but this seems like a missed opportunity. There are important dialogues to be had about social, ethical and political issues that are well suited to be discussed in relation to artworks, and in relation to historical attitudes towards art, i.e. if we consider who was allowed into or excluded from the art academy, from being displayed in art galleries, and even what style/s and subject/s of art were deemed appropriate for artists to render. These educational opportunities are interesting, engaging and have a wider relevance to the world. If the art teacher chooses to forgo and avoid such themes and conversations in relation to artworks and their associated aesthetic experiences, this means that students may not gain valuable skills of critical spectatorship required to engage with the multiple and varied arts. Failing to gain such skills does not then protect students when they are out on their own, encountering, engaging with and stumbling upon other artworks, particularly contemporary works that include mass art and media. Thus, the skill of learning to appreciate and engage both critically and in a receptive or sympathetic manner with artworks is of fundamental use to our students throughout their lives.

Conclusion: The necessity of aesthetic education

Art is not a luxury. Can you even imagine a world inhabited by humans in which art does not exist? Aesthetic expression and experience has always been an integral aspect to what it means to be human. We have developed increasingly sophisticated ways to share ideas, communicate, and make meaning together as social creatures. One key way we express our experiences of life is through rendering them in multimedia to display and share with others so that the objects we create may invoke in those receptive to it the same experience we encountered at a certain moment in a specific setting. This sharing of experience, rendered aesthetically, unites us, helps us to understand ourselves, one another and the environment in which we exist.

Such creative artistic expressions and their associated aesthetic experiences therefore must be connected to a socio-politico-economic-ethical context because we are social, political, ethical beings: this is unavoidable. Audre Lorde (1977 [2017]: 4) writes:

> Poetry is not a luxury. ... The white fathers told us: I think, therefore I am. The Black mother within each of us – the poet – whispers in our dreams: I feel, therefore I can be free. Poetry coins the language to express and charter this revolutionary demand, the implementation of that freedom.

How can we not speak with our own voice, imbued with our experiences, that resonates with others, or is handed over as a gift to be interpreted and hopefully appreciated? Art has historically been connected with religious devotion and belief, but Martha Nussbaum (1998b: 59) remarks that '[t]he arts show us that we can have order and discipline and meaning and logic from within ourselves: we do not have to choose between belief in god and empty chaos'.

Not all art is good. Some art is lacking, in terms of the artist's skill, technique, appropriate sensitivity or ethical awareness. Some art may hit differently at various moments in time. Much art is radical, revolutionary, politically charged and aims at creating change, pushing boundaries, expanding horizons. Yet artists have also been instrumental in being employed to maintain a certain kind of status quo of ideals and standards (consider, for example, the commissioned religious artworks that were determined in a specific style and featured sanctioned images and content that were designed to subscribe and police specific social, religious and ethical mores). The skill of the artist, the presentation or display of the artwork as well as the reception of the work, which includes the viewer's attitude, each of these aspects benefits from forms of critical and technical learning, training, practice and education. There is a necessity for aesthetic education because art is valuable and it is powerful: it is aesthetically valuable as well as valuable for many additional reasons besides. Artworks and the practice of artists may also be instrumentally valuable: ethically valuable; politically valuable; it may have social and individual benefits (or possible drawbacks), and it is also economically valuable.

Of these various benefits that may be gained from artworks – from the creation and reception of art objects – it is vital that we understand the essential role art plays in the human life. As a fully human rather than merely animalistic life, we seek to fulfil our central human capabilities, including the use of our senses, imagination and thought. The well-lived life includes the functioning of all the central human capabilities, including their creative and artistic use, and it necessarily includes aesthetic experiences. Given artworks are distinctly created in order to convey such aesthetic experiences, they play a vital role in connecting human beings to such aesthetic experiences, which, in turn, are constitutive of the flourishing, meaningful or well-lived life.

In this way, it is the intrinsic value of art that supports the necessity of aesthetic education in schools. Education aims at providing some of the foundations for the good life. This includes but is not limited to providing children and young people with knowledge, a supportive environment that helps them to cultivate good habits such as the virtues, being reasonable, and learning to share and tolerate others who may be different from us. Schools meet some of the basic needs of children as well as some of the human capabilities, including, for instance, play. Schools play a vital role in setting children up to be autonomous decision makers who in their adult lives can choose what they wish to do, and how and why. It is not being suggested that schools and teachers are solely responsible for the health and well-being – let alone future flourishing – of children and young people: there are obviously other significant people and institutions in the lives of children and young people who are also integral to the care-taking required to ensure that individuals are adequately grounded in aspects of the good life.

Kristján Kristjánsson (2020: 1) claims:

> Student flourishing (understood as students' objective well-being) [is] the overarching aim of education. Because I consider good education to be part of the good life, rather than just preparation for it, I need to engage with a broad conception of human flourishing and show how education, ideally, both initiates and encourages it …. *Human flourishing* is the (relatively) unencumbered, freely chosen and developmentally progressive activity of a meaningful (subjectively purposeful and objectively valuable) life that actualises satisfactorily an individual human being's natural capacities in areas of species-specific existential tasks at which human beings (as rational, social, moral and emotional agents) can most successfully excel.

As Kristjánsson argues, then, the overarching aim of education is flourishing. And, emergent from this argument, as I have excavated and justified in this book, is the understanding that aesthetic experiences are an element of the flourishing life. It would be doing these young people an injustice if we did not expose them to the understanding and experiences available to them that they may enjoy, seek out, create and share awe-filled, wondrous, moving and momentous experiences derived from the multiple and various arts. As educators we have a duty and a responsibility to induct young people into the history of art that has been around for as long as our oldest living human cultures, and share with them that they are able to participate in arts making and reception: in aesthetic experiences.

It is not enough for people to know that aesthetic experiences exist: being appropriately inducted into them through the arts is important. We have an innate human instinct for art and for aesthetic experiences, but this does not mean we will all necessarily be easily able to access and understand the variety of aesthetic experiences there to be gleaned from the multiple and various arts. We need to be well educated to receive artworks critically and sympathetically. Art surrounds us, and with a proper initiation via art teachers, we will be better at interpreting, critiquing and being open to receiving and creating the messages, meanings and feelings conveyed through art. As such, this book defends the necessity of aesthetic education for all school-aged students, on the basis of the distinctive *aesthetic value* that art holds: the capacity to offer and create an aesthetic experience for those who appropriately engage with it.

My account sees the value of art as intrinsic: we engage with or create and enjoy the artwork for its own sake, for the sake of the experience it affords, rather than for the sake of anything else. Even if I want to make a career out of some artistic or creative pursuit, and earn a living from these artistic skills, ultimately I enjoy the making of art and the reception of artworks because they are worthwhile activities in and of themselves. Aesthetic experiences are intrinsically valuable and worthwhile, and they are also constitutive of the flourishing life – *eudaimonia* – a fully human life. Given we as educators wish to prepare our students for a meaningful, satisfactory life – our overarching aim is student flourishing – this means that we aim at a life which includes such wondrous aesthetic experiences (among other things).

Therefore, in order to teach young people that they are able to seek out and undergo such incredible experiences, ones that augment one's life, we ought to teach them about the arts – about the historical and theoretical aspects as well as the practical and technical aspects. They must be taught aesthetic education. The educational aspect of this argument is important because while young people may naturally stumble upon arts and crafts, making and appreciating the multiple arts require specific skills. Such skills include the open, receptive, sympathetic and yet also critical attitude required to engage with artworks so as to invoke the relevant aesthetic experiences there to be had. These skills, attitudes and dispositions are more likely to be accessible, to be made manifest if they are cultivated, supported and encouraged by being taught and learned as well as practised.

The art class in a school environment that is well resourced and valued, including in terms of its teacher and the curriculum, is the best way to ensure every child has this opportunity to learn about and develop such skills. Aesthetic education, therefore, is required if we are serious about the overarching aim of education, and of life, to be *eudaimonia* or flourishing, or a life that is 'subjectively purposeful and objectively valuable', as Kristjánsson clarifies.

I have proclaimed *The Necessity of Aesthetic Education* is a manifesto. Let them have aesthetic experiences! Provide them with aesthetic education! If education is to prepare students for a flourishing life, it must expose students to art making and appreciation and teach them that the enjoyment the arts have to offer is an option available for them to choose to include in their lives. If aesthetic experiences are to become a readily accessible component of their lives, students must be taught how to *experience* art. This involves valuing art for its own sake: for the purpose for which it is created; namely, to evoke an aesthetic experience in the receiver of the artwork. In this book I have detailed and defended a philosophical argument for the necessity of aesthetic education for all school-aged students, from pre-primary to high school, on the basis of the distinctive value of the arts and the role of aesthetic experience in the flourishing life.

Notes

Chapter 1

1. In the UK, disadvantaged students are usually defined as such according to their family socio-economic status. For instance, such students are often eligible for free school meals. The educational performance of pupils from disadvantaged backgrounds is much lower than their peers, leading to what is often called an attainment or achievement gap (OECD, 2012).
2. The Commission on the Arts is a million-dollar-funded art project organized through the American Academy of Arts & Sciences examining the role of the arts in American life, with emphasis on education and infrastructure. The project chairs are John A. Lithgow, Deborah F. Rutter and Natasha D. Trethewey.

Chapter 2

1. This is not to say that all art objects or objects that produce an aesthetic experience must be pleasant or beautiful.
2. Note that for Collingwood, craft is not art proper precisely because it does not express a distinct or unique emotion. Similarly, mass artworks such as films are criticized by expressivists such as Dwight MacDonald as pseudo-art because they offer generic or 'canned' emotional experiences rather than unique, distinctive expressions such as that afforded by art proper: namely high art or avant-garde art (see Carroll, 1998b).
3. Note: there are other reasons Broudy provides instead in order to defend arts education as foundational, but these have to do with the social role art plays in society (1991: 132).

Chapter 4

1. Currently 55 per cent of the world's population live in cities, with the United Nations estimating that by the 2050s more than two-thirds of us will live in urban rather than country environments.

2   Some more than others. Mass art (such as blockbuster movies from Hollywood or Bollywood) notoriously aims at the largest possible untutored audience as it is accessible and easy to understand usually on first viewing (Carroll, 1998b; D'Olimpio, 2018).

3   Note that Dickie (1964) and Kemp (1999: 393) deny or ignore that the form of attention in question be 'sympathetic'.

4   This is not to deny that receivers of artworks will also respond subjectively to artworks and sometimes feel what is not intended by the artist or necessarily depicted in the formal features of the work. I shall set aside the debate about 'ideal' readings of artworks and the 'intentional fallacy' (Wimsatt & Beardsley, 1946) for now.

5   Movements such as 'everyday aesthetics' (Saito, 2007) have emerged from Dewey's (1934) pragmatic conception of the arts and see aesthetic experience as an extension of ordinary experience.

6   The word 'potentially' here refers to the fact that some babies or young children may die before they have had the chance to grow and developmentally acquire the capacity for such expression, appreciation and understanding. It also refers to the fact that some severely disabled people may never manifest such capability despite potentially possessing it *qua* human beings.

7   Hirst (1973) defends literature and the fine arts as offering a unique form of aesthetic knowledge. This argument is critiqued by Pring (1976) and Wilson (1979) and discussed in Hand (2006).

8   Autonomous adults may choose a lifestyle that lacks fulfilment or functioning of some of the central human capabilities and to this extent they may not experience *eudaimonia*. Whether or not a life is deemed to have been flourishing may be determined upon consideration of the whole life lived.

Chapter 5

1   In fact, Reiss and White (2013: 17) claim that 'Pulp fiction, soap operas, and B movies are also about human life and relationships. Their authors and directors know all about getting an audience hooked. But we rightly do not rate them highly as educational vehicles. Indeed, we sometimes see them as anti-educational – if, for instance, they reinforce stereotypes, rather than challenge them.'

2   For instance, Reiss and White (2013) refer to personal qualities, whereas Brighouse et al. (2018) refer to personal autonomy and personal fulfilment. Note: allowing for individual differences does not undermine normativity.

Chapter 7

1. Noël Carroll outlines the different aesthetic positions that may be held with regard to art, including his own 'moderate moralism' in 'Art and Ethical Criticism: an overview of recent directions of research', *Ethics* 110:2 (2000): 350–87. See also 'Ethical Criticism of Art' in the *Internet Encyclopedia of Philosophy*, available from https://www.iep.utm.edu/art-eth/#SH5a
2. I am using the words 'moral' and 'ethical' interchangeably.
3. See debates within the public domain such as 'Can bad people create good art', *Radio National Books and Arts* (28 November 2016). Retrieved via: http://www.abc.net.au/radionational/programs/booksandarts/can-bad-people-create-good-art/8059032 and Antony Funnell's 'Our favourite paedophile: Why is Donald Friend still celebrated?' *ABC* (2 February 2017). Retrieved via: http://www.abc.net.au/news/2016-11-28/donald-friend-our-favourite-paedophile/8053222

References

Adajian, T. (2018). The Definition of Art. In E. N. Zalta (Ed.). *The Stanford Encyclopedia of Philosophy*. Retrieved from https://plato.stanford.edu/archives/fall2018/entries/art-definition/. Accessed 7 May 2020.

American Academy of Arts & Sciences (14 September 2021). Press Release: New Report Makes the Case for Arts Education: Recommends Access for All. Retrieved from https://www.amacad.org/news/arts-education-report

Aristotle (1876). *The Nicomachean Ethics*. London: Longmans, Green.

Arnheim, R. (1969). *Visual Thinking*. Berkeley: University of California Press.

Arts Council England (April 2019). Arts Council England's Response to the Office for Standards in Education, Children's Services and Skills Education Inspection Framework 2019: Inspecting the Substance of Education Consultation. Retrieved from https://www.artscouncil.org.uk/sites/default/files/download-file/Arts%20 Council%20Englands%20response%20to%20Ofsteds%20Education%20 inspection%20framework%202019%20Consultation.pdf

Australia Council for the Arts (2002). *Support for the Arts Handbook*. Strawberry Hills: Australia Council for the Arts.

Australian Curriculum, Assessment and Reporting Authority (2011). The Australian Curriculum: General Capabilities. Retrieved from https://www.australiancurriculum.edu.au/f-10-curriculum/general-capabilities/

Australian Curriculum, Assessment and Reporting Authority (2014). The Arts. Retrieved from https://www.australiancurriculum.edu.au/f-10-curriculum/the-arts/introduction/. Accessed 8 May 2020.

Baker, N. (11 December 2019). Government Defends Axing Arts Department as a 'Good Opportunity' for Artists. *SBS News*. Retrieved from https://www.sbs.com.au/news/article/government-defends-axing-arts-department-as-a-good-opportunity-for-artists/psnturigl. Accessed 8 August 2023.

Baker, N. (6 December 2019). 'Massive Backwards Step': Australia to No Longer Have a Federal Arts Department. *SBS News*. Retrieved from https://www.sbs.com.au/news/massive-backwards-step-australia-to-no-longer-have-a-federal-arts-department. Accessed 6 May 2020.

Bamford, A. (2006). *The Wow Factor: Global Research Compendium on the Impact of the Arts in Education*. Münster: Waxmann Verlag.

Barone, T. & Eisner, E. W. (2011). *Arts Based Research*. New York: Sage Publishing.

Barton, G. & Baguley, M. (2017). *The Palgrave Handbook of Global Arts Education*. London: Palgrave Macmillan.

Beardsley, M. (1958). *Aesthetics: Problems in the Philosophy of Criticism*. New York: Harcourt, Brace.
Beardsley, M. (1982). *The Aesthetic Point of View: Selected Essays*. M. Wreen & D. Callen (Eds.). Ithaca: Cornell University Press.
Bell, C. (1915). *Art*. London: Chatto and Windus.
Best, D. (1992). *The Rationality of Feeling: Understanding the Arts in Education*. London: Falmer Press.
Biesta, G. (2017). *Letting Art Teach: Art Education 'after' Joseph Beuys*. Arnhem: Artez Press.
Bohlin, K. (2005). *Teaching Character Education through Literature: Awakening the Moral Imagination in Secondary Classrooms*. New York: Routledge.
Booth, W. C. (1988). *The Company We Keep: An Ethics of Fiction*. Los Angeles, CA: University of California Press.
Booth, W. C. (1998). Why Banning Ethical Criticism Is a Serious Mistake. *Philosophy and Literature*, 22(2): 366-93.
Bresler, L. (Ed.) (2007). *International Handbook of Research in Arts Education*. Dordrecht: Springer.
Brighouse, H. (2006). *On Education (Thinking in Action)*. New York: Routledge.
Brighouse, H., Ladd, H. F., Loeb, S., & Swift, A. (2018). *Educational Goods: Values, Evidence, and Decision-Making*. Chicago: University of Chicago Press.
Broudy, H. S. (1991). The Arts as Basic Education. In R. A. Smith & A. Simpson (Eds.). *Aesthetics and Arts Education*. Chicago: University of Illinois Press, 125-33.
Broudy, H. S. (1994/1972). *Enlightened Cherishing: An Essay in Aesthetic Education*. Urbana: University of Illinois Press.
Bullough, E. (1977). *Aesthetics*. Westport, CT: Greenwood Press.
California State Board of Education (2004). *Visual and Performing Arts Framework for California Public Schools: Kindergarten through Grade Twelve*. Sacramento: California Department of Education. Retrieved from https://www.cde.ca.gov/ci/cr/cf/documents/vpaframewrk.pdf. Accessed 24 June 2020.
Carr, D. (2005). On the Contribution of Literature and the Arts to the Educational Cultivation of Moral Virtue, Feeling and Emotion. *Journal of Moral Education*, 34(2): 137-51.
Carr, D. (2017). Literature, Rival Conceptions of Virtue, and Moral Education. *The Journal of Aesthetic Education*, 51(2): 1-16.
Carr, D. & Harrison, T. (2015). *Educating Character through Stories*. Exeter: Imprint Academic.
Carroll, N. (1996). Moderate Moralism. *British Journal of Aesthetics*, 36: 223-37.
Carroll, N. (1998a). Moderate Moralism versus Moderate Autonomism. *British Journal of Aesthetics*, 38: 419-24.
Carroll, N. (1998b). *A Philosophy of Mass Art*. Oxford: Clarendon Press.
Carroll, N. (2000). Art and Ethical Criticism: An Overview of Recent Directions of Research. *Ethics*, 110(2): 350-87.

Carroll, N. (2001). *Beyond Aesthetics: Philosophical Essays*. Cambridge: Cambridge University Press.

Cavell, S. (1988). *In Quest of the Ordinary: Lines of Scepticism and Romanticism*. Chicago: Chicago University Press.

Chapman, S., Wright, P. R., & Pascoe, R. (2018a). Arts Curriculum Implementation: 'Adopt and Adapt' as Policy Translation. *Arts Education Policy Review*, 119(1): 12–24. https://doi.org/10.1080/10632913.2016.1201031

Chapman, S., Wright, P. R., & Pascoe, R. (2018b). Content without Context Is Noise: Looking for Curriculum Harmony in Primary Arts Education in Western Australia. *International Journal of Education & the Arts*, 19(2): 1–25. Retrieved from http://www.ijea.org/v19n2/index.html. Accessed 11 December 2023.

Cohen, R. (2019). Arts Facts: Arts and Cultural Production Percentage of GDP 2019. *Americans for the Arts*. Retrieved from https://www.americansforthearts.org/by-program/reports-and-data/legislation-policy/naappd/arts-and-cultural-production-percentage-of-gdp. Accessed 18 February 2023.

Collingwood, R. G. (1938). *The Principles of Art*. Oxford: Clarendon Press.

Collinson, D. (1992). Aesthetic Experience. In O. Hanfling (Ed.). *Philosophical Aesthetics: An Introduction*. Oxford: Blackwell, 111–78.

Conway, C. M., Hibbard, S., Albert, D., & Hourigan, R. (2005). Professional Development for Arts Teachers. *Arts Education Policy Review*, 107(1): 3–10. https://doi.org/10.3200/AEPR.107.1.3-10

Craig, C. J., Li, J., & Kelley, M. (2022). 'Charting Waters of New Seas': The Scholarly Contributions of Elliot Eisner. *Journal of Curriculum Studies*, 54(2): 147–64. https://doi.org/10.1080/00220272.2021.1927193

Creative Industries Trade and Investment Board, UK (December 2022). Putting the UK's Creative Industries Centre Stage: An International Strategy for the Creative Industries 2022–2025. Retrieved from https://wecreate.org.nz/wp-content/uploads/2023/02/CITIB-Strategy-Report_2022-FINAL-Dec6.pdf. Accessed 20 February 2023.

Cunningham, S. (23 May 2022). The Creative Economy in Australia. *Committee for Economic Development of Australia*. Opinion Article. Retrieved from https://www.ceda.com.au/NewsAndResources/Opinion/Arts-Sports-Culture/The-creative-economy-in-Australia. Accessed 20 February 2023.

Danto, A. (1978). The Artworld. In J. Margolis (Ed.). *Philosophy Looks at the Arts*. Philadelphia: Temple University Press, 154–67.

Danto, A. (1981). *The Transfiguration of the Commonplace: A Philosophy of Art*. Cambridge: Harvard University Press.

Davidson, D. (2001). *Subjective, Intersubjective, Objective*. Oxford: Oxford University Press.

Devereaux, M. (1998). Beauty and Evil: The Case of Leni Riefenstahl's Triumph of the Will. In J. Levinson (Ed.). *Aesthetics and Ethics: Essays at the Intersection*. New York: Cambridge University Press.

Devereaux, M. (2004). Moral Judgements and Works of Art: The Case of Narrative Literature. *The Journal of Aesthetics and Art Criticism*, 62(1): 3–11.

Dewey, J. (1934/1980). *Art as Experience*. New York: Perigee.
DfE (2013a). Statutory Guidance: National Curriculum in England: Art and Design programmes of Study. Retrieved from https://www.gov.uk/government/publications/national-curriculum-in-england-art-and-design-programmes-of-study. Accessed 6 May 2020.
DfE (2013b). Statutory Guidance: National Curriculum in England: Music Programmes of Study. Retrieved from https://www.gov.uk/government/publications/national-curriculum-in-england-music-programmes-of-study/national-curriculum-in-england-music-programmes-of-study. Accessed 6 May 2020.
Dickie, G. (1964). The Myth of the Aesthetic Attitude. *American Philosophical Quarterly*, 1(1): 54–64.
Dickie, G. (1974). *Art and the Aesthetic: An Institutional Analysis*. Ithaca: Cornell University Press.
Dickie, G. (1983). *Aesthetics: A Critical Anthology*. New York: St Martin's Press.
D'Olimpio, L. (2014). Thoughts on Film: Critically Engaging with Both Adorno and Benjamin. *Educational Philosophy and Theory*, 47(6): 622–37.
D'Olimpio, L. (3 June 2016). The Trolley Dilemma: Would You Kill One Person to Save Five? *The Conversation*.
D'Olimpio, L. (2018). *Media and Moral Education: A Philosophy of Critical Engagement*. London: Routledge.
D'Olimpio, L. (2020a). When Good Art Is Bad: Educating the Critical Viewer. *Theory and Research in Education*, 18(2): 137–50. https://doi.org/10.1177/1477878520947024
D'Olimpio, L. (2020b). Education and the Arts: Inspiring Wonder. In A. Schinkel (Ed.). *Wonder, Education and Human Flourishing*. Amsterdam: Vrije Universiteit University Press, 256–70.
D'Olimpio, L. (2021). Defending Aesthetic Education. *British Journal of Educational Studies*, 70(3): 263–79. https://doi.org/10.1080/00071005.2021.1960267
D'Olimpio, L. (2022). Aesthetica and *Eudaimonia*: Education for Flourishing Must Include the Arts. *Journal of Philosophy of Education*, 56(2): 238–50. https://doi.org/10.1111/1467-9752.12661
D'Olimpio, L., Paris, P., & Thompson, A. P. (Eds.) (2022). *Educating Character through the Arts*. London: Routledge.
D'Olimpio, L. & Peterson, A. (2018). The Ethics of Narrative Art: Philosophy in Schools, Compassion and Learning from Stories. *Journal of Philosophy in Schools*, 5(1): 92–110.
Dutton, D. (2009). *The Art Instinct: Beauty, Pleasure and Human Evolution*. New York: Bloomsbury Press.
Eaton, M. M. (1989). *Aesthetics and the Good Life*. Rutherford: Farleigh Dickinson University Press.
Eaton, M. M. (2001). *Merit, Aesthetic and Ethical*. Oxford: Oxford University Press.
Eaton, M. M. & Moore, R. (2002). Aesthetic Experience: Its Revival and Its Relevance to Aesthetic Education. *The Journal of Aesthetic Education*, 36(2): 9–23.

Egan, K., Cant, A., & Judson, G. (Eds.) (2014). *Wonder-full Education: The Centrality of Wonder in Teaching and Learning across the Curriculum*. New York: Routledge.

Egan, K. & Gajdamaschko, N. (2003). Some Cognitive Tools of Literacy. In A. Kozulin (Ed.). *Vygotsky's Educational Theory in Cultural Context*. Cambridge: Cambridge University Press, 83–98.

Eisner, E. (1979). *The Educational Imagination: On the Design and Evaluation of School Programs*. New York: Macmillan.

Eisner, E. (1981). The Role of the Arts in Cognition and Curriculum. *The Phi Delta Kappan*, 63(1): 48–52. Retrieved from https://www.jstor.org/stable/20386160

Eisner, E. (1990). Discipline-based Art Education: Conceptions and Misconceptions. *Educational Theory*, 40(4): 423–30. https://doi.org/10.1111/j.1741-5446.1990.00423.x

Eisner, E. (1992). The Misunderstood Role of the Arts in Human Development. *The Phi Delta Kappan*, 73(8): 591–5. Retrieved from http://myfcscourses.com/3270/FCS_3270_2_files/Arts%20and%20human%20development.pdf

Eisner, E. (1996). *Cognition and Curriculum Reconsidered*. London: Paul Chapman Publishing Ltd.

Eisner, E. (2002a). *The Arts and the Creation of Mind*. New Haven: Yale University Press.

Eisner, E. (2002b). From Episteme to Phronesis to Artistry in the Study and Improvement of Teaching. *Teaching and Teacher Education*, 18(4): 375–85.

Eisner, E. (2002c). The Kind of Schools We Need. *The Phi Delta Kappan*, 83(8): 576–83.

Eisner, E. (2005). *Reimagining Schools: The Selected Works of Elliot W. Eisner*. London: Routledge.

Eisner, E. (2009). The Lowenfeld Lecture 2008: What Education Can Learn from the Arts. *Art Education*, 62(2): 6–9.

Eisner, E. & Day, M. (Eds.) (2004, 2008). *Handbook of Research and Policy in Art Education*. London: Lawrence Erlbaum Associates, 2004. Reprinted London: Taylor & Francis, 2008.

Eldridge, R. (2003). *An Introduction to the Philosophy of Art*. Cambridge: Cambridge University Press.

Elliot, R. K. (2006). *Aesthetics, Imagination, and the Unity of Experience*. P. Crowther (Ed.). Hampshire: Ashgate.

Ewing, R. (2010). *The Arts and Australian Education: Realising Potential*. ACER (Australian Council for Educational Research). Camberwell: ACER Press.

Ewing, R. (2020). The Australian Curriculum. The Arts. A Critical Opportunity. *Curriculum Perspectives*, 40: 75–81. https://doi.org/10.1007/s41297-019-00098-w

Frankena, W. K. (1973). *Ethics*. Second edition, Englewood Cliffs: Prentice Hall.

Freedman, J. (1993). *Professions of Taste: Henry James, British Aestheticism, and Commodity Culture*. California: Stanford University Press.

Fry, R. (1920). *Vision and Design*. London: Chatto & Windus.

Funnell, A. (28 November 2016). Can Bad People Create Good Art. *Radio National Books and Arts for the Australian Broadcasting Corporation (ABC)*. Retrieved from http://www.abc.net.au/radionational/programs/booksandarts/can-bad-people-create-good-art/8059032

Funnell, A. (2 February 2017). Our Favourite Paedophile: Why Is Donald Friend Still Celebrated? *Australian Broadcasting Corporation (ABC)*. Retrieved from http://www.abc.net.au/news/2016-11-28/donald-friend-our-favourite-paedophile/8053222

Gadamer, H.-G. (1986). *The Relevance of the Beautiful and Other Essays* (Trans.: N. Walker and Ed.: R. Bernasconi). Cambridge: Cambridge University Press.

Gaut, B. (1998). The Ethical Criticism of Art. In J. Levinson (Ed.). *Aesthetics and Ethics*. Cambridge: Cambridge University Press, 182–203.

Gibbons, A. (17 December 2019). Call to Include Visual Art in Core National Curriculum. *TES*. Retrieved from https://www.tes.com/news/call-include-visual-art-core-national-curriculum. 1 May 2020.

Gibson, R. & Anderson, M. (2008). Touching the Void: Arts Education Research in Australia. *Asia Pacific Journal of Education*, 28(1): 103–12. https://doi.org/10.1080/02188790701849818

Gingell, J. (2006). *The Visual Arts and Education*. IMPACT Pamphlet. Issue 13. London: Wiley. Retrieved from https://onlinelibrary.wiley.com/doi/epdf/10.1111/j.2048-416X.2006.tb00109.x

Gombrich, E. (1963). *Meditations on a Hobbyhorse and Other Essays on the Theory of Art*. London: Phaidon.

Goodman, N. (1976). *Languages of Art: An Approach to a Theory of Symbols*. Cambridge: Hackett.

Granger, D. A. (2006). *John Dewey, Robert Pirsig, and the Art of Living: Revisioning Aesthetic Education*. New York: Palgrave Macmillan.

Greene, M. (1977). The Artistic – Aesthetic and Curriculum. *Curriculum Inquiry*, 6(4): 283–96.

Greene, M. (1978). *Landscapes of Learning*. New York: Teachers College Press.

Greene, M. (1995). *Releasing the Imagination: Essays on Education, the Arts and Social Change*. San Francisco: Jossey Bass.

Greene, M. (2001). *Variations on a Blue Guitar: The Lincoln Center Institute Lectures on Aesthetic Education*. New York: Teachers College Press, Columbia University.

Guhn, M., Emerson, S. D., & Gouzouasis, P. (2019). A Population-level Analysis of Associations between School Music Participation and Academic Achievement. *Journal of Educational Psychology*, 112(2): 308–28. https://doi.org/10.1037/edu0000376

Hand, M. (2006). *Is Religious Education Possible?* London: Bloomsbury.

Hand, M. (2010). On the Worthwhileness of Theoretical Activities. *Journal of Philosophy of Education*, 43(10): 109–21.

Hanfling, O. (Ed.), (1992). *Philosophical Aesthetics: An Introduction*. Oxford: Blackwell.

Haynes, F. (2017). Aesthetic Education. *Encyclopedia of Educational Philosophy and Theory*. Singapore: Springer. Retrieved from https://link.springer.com/referenceworkentry/10.1007/978-981-287-588-4_292. Accessed 28 April 2020.

Heller, S. (1998). Wearying of Cultural Studies, Some Scholars Rediscover Beauty. *Colloquy in Chronicle of Higher Education*. http://chronicle.com/article/Wearying-of-Cultural-Studies/35418/

Hepburn, R. W. (1980). The Inaugural Address: Wonder. *Proceedings of the Aristotelian Society, Supplementary Volumes*, 54: 1–23.

Hill, L. (29 May 2018). Exclusive: Collapse in GCSE Arts Subjects Gathers Pace. *Arts Professional*. Retrieved from https://www.artsprofessional.co.uk/news/exclusive-collapse-gcse-arts-subjects-gathers-pace

Hirst, P. H. (1973). Literature and the Fine Arts as a Unique Form of Knowledge. *Cambridge Journal of Education*, 3(3): 118–32.

HM Government (2002). *Education Act 2002*. Retrieved from https://www.legislation.gov.uk/ukpga/2002/32/contents

Iseminger, G. (2003). Aesthetic Experience. In J. Levinson (Ed.). *The Oxford Handbook of Aesthetics*. Oxford: Oxford University Press, 99–116.

Jackson, F. (1986). What Mary Didn't Know. *Journal of Philosophy*, 83: 291–5.

Judson, G. & Egan, K. (2012). Elliot Eisner's Imagination and Learning. *Journal of Curriculum and Pedagogy*, 9(1): 38–41. https://doi.org/10.1080/15505170.2012.684845

Kaelin, E. F. (1989). *An Aesthetics for Educators*. New York: Teachers College Press.

Kamal, S. & Bierman, N. (18 August 2017). 16 Members of White House Arts Panel Resign to Protest Trump's Response to Charlottesville. *Los Angeles Times*. Retrieved from https://www.latimes.com/politics/washington/la-na-essential-washington-updates-201708-htmlstory.html#all-17-members-of-white-house-arts-panel-resign-to-protest-trumps-response-to-charlottesville. Accessed 20 April 2020.

Kant, I. (1785). *Grundlegung zur Metaphysik der Sitten*. Translated as *Groundwork of the Metaphysics of Morals*. In M. Gregor (Trans. and Ed.). *Immanuel Kant: Practical Philosophy*. Cambridge: Cambridge University Press, 37–108.

Kearns, L. (2015). Subjects of Wonder: Toward an Aesthetics, Ethics, and Pedagogy of Wonder. *The Journal of Aesthetic Education*, 49(1): 98–119.

Kelly, M. (Ed.) (1998). *Encyclopedia of Aesthetics*. New York: Oxford University Press.

Kemp, G. (1999). The Aesthetic Attitude. *British Journal of Aesthetics*, 39(4): 392–9.

Kisida, B. & Bowen, D. H. (12 February 2019). New Evidence of the Benefits of Arts Education. *Brown Center Chalkboard. The Brookings Institution*. Retrieved from https://www.brookings.edu/blog/brown-center-chalkboard/2019/02/12/new-evidence-of-the-benefits-of-arts-education/. Accessed 29 June 2020.

Klein, N. (2010). *No Logo*. New York: Picador.

Klein, N. (2014). *This Changes Everything: Capitalism vs. the Climate*. New York: Simon & Schuster.

Knott, J. (5 July 2018). Arts Teacher Numbers Plummet by Almost a Quarter. *Arts Professional*. Retrieved from https://www.artsprofessional.co.uk/news/arts-teacher-numbers-plummet-almost-quarter. Accessed 10 May 2020.

Koopman, C. (2005). Art as Fulfilment: On the Justification of Education in the Arts. *Journal of Philosophy of Education*, 39(1): 85–97.

Kristjánsson, K. (2016). Flourishing as the Aim of Education: Towards an Extended, 'Enchanted' Aristotelian Account. *Oxford Review of Education*, 42(6): 707–20.

Kristjánsson, K. (2017). Recent Work on Flourishing as the Aim of Education: A Critical Review. *British Journal of Educational Studies*, 65(1): 87–107.

Kristjánsson, K. (2020). *Flourishing as the Aim of Education: A Neo-Aristotelian View*. London: Routledge.

Ladkin, S., McKay, R., & Bojesen, E. (2016). *Against Value in the Arts and Education*. London: Rowman and Littlefield International.

Lake, R. (Ed.) (2010). *Dear Maxine: Letters from the Unfinished Conversation with Maxine Greene*. New York: Columbia University, Teachers College Press.

Levinson, J. (2004a). Defining Art Historically. In P. Lamarque & S. H. Olsen (Eds.). *Aesthetics and the Philosophy of Art: The Analytic Tradition*. Oxford: Blackwell, 35–46.

Levinson, J. (2004b). Intention and Interpretation in Literature. In P. Lamarque & S. H. Olsen (Eds.). *Aesthetics and the Philosophy of Art: The Analytic Tradition*. Oxford: Blackwell, 200–22.

Levinson, J. (Ed.) (2001). *Aesthetics and Ethics: Essays at the Intersection*. Cambridge: Cambridge University Press.

Lewis, C. S. (1961). *An Experiment in Criticism*. Cambridge: Cambridge University Press.

Lloyd, G. (2018). *Reclaiming Wonder: After the Sublime*. Edinburgh: Edinburgh University Press.

Lorde, A. (1977/2017). Poetry Is Not a Luxury. In *The Master's Tools Will Never Dismantle the Master's House*. London: Penguin Modern, 23: 1–5.

MacIntyre, A. (2007). *After Virtue: A Study in Moral Theory*. Indiana: University of Notre Dame Press.

Magee, B. (1978). Philosophy and Literature: Dialogue with Iris Murdoch. In *Men of Ideas*. London: British Broadcasting Corporation (BBC).

McCarthy, K., Ondaatje, E., Zakaras, L., & Brooks, A. (2004). Gifts of the Muse: Reframing the Debate about the Benefits of the Arts. Santa Monica, CA: RAND. Retrieved from https://www.rand.org/pubs/monographs/MG218.html

McGill, E., Eckstein, A., & Stringer, S. M. (April 2014). State of the Arts: A Plan to Boost Arts Education in New York City Schools. *Office of the New York City Comptroller*. Retrieved from http://comptroller.nyc.gov/

Mill, J. S. (1861). *Utilitarianism*. References by chapter and paragraph number. Full text available online via Oxford World's Classics.

Moore, R. (1998). History of Aesthetic Education. In *Encyclopedia of Aesthetics*. Vol. 2. New York: Oxford University Press, 89–93.

Moore, R. (Ed.) (1995). *Aesthetics for Young People*. Reston, VA: National Art Education Association.

Murdoch, I. (1970). *The Sovereignty of Good*. London: Routledge.

Murdoch, I. (1998). *Existentialists and Mystics: Writings on Philosophy and Literature*. P. J. Conradi (Ed.). New York: Allen Lane/The Penguin Press.

Nabokov, V. (1955). *Lolita*. Paris: Olympia Press.

National Endowment for the Arts (30 March 2021). New Report Released on the Economic Impact of the Arts and Cultural Sector: 2019 Data Analyzed by National Endowment for the Arts and Bureau of Economic Analysis Shows Sector Growth before Pandemic. Retrieved from https://www.arts.gov/news/press-releases/2021/new-report-released-economic-impact-arts-and-cultural-sector. Accessed 18 February 2023.

Noddings, N. (2012). The Eisner Legacy: A Warning Unheeded. *Journal of Curriculum and Pedagogy*, 9(1): 29–31. https://doi.org/10.1080/15505170.2012.684841

Nussbaum, M. C. (1990). *Love's Knowledge: Essays on Philosophy and Literature*. Oxford: Oxford University Press.

Nussbaum, M. C. (1998a). Exactly and Responsibly: A Defence of Ethical Criticism. *Philosophy and Literature*, 22: 343–65.

Nussbaum, M. C. (1998b). The Transfigurations of Intoxication: Nietzsche, Schopenhauer and Dionysus. In S. Kemal, I. Gaskell & D. W. Conway (Eds.). *Nietzsche, Philosophy and the Arts*. Cambridge: Cambridge University Press, 36–69.

Nussbaum, M. C. (2000). *Women and Human Development: The Capabilities Approach*. Cambridge: Cambridge University Press.

Nussbaum, M. C. (2001). *Upheavals of Thought: The Intelligence of Emotions*. Cambridge: Cambridge University Press.

Nussbaum, M. C. (2006). *Frontiers of Justice: Disability, Nationality, Species Membership*. Cambridge, MA: Belknap Press.

Nussbaum, M. C. (2010). *Not for Profit: Why Democracy Needs the Humanities*. Princeton, NJ: Princeton University Press.

Nussbaum, M. C. (2011). *Creating Capabilities: The Human Development Approach*. Cambridge, MA: Belknap Press of Harvard University Press.

OECD (2012). *Equity and Quality in Education: Supporting Disadvantaged Students and Schools*. Paris: OECD Publishing. Retrieved from http://dx.doi.org/10.1787/9789264130852-en

O'Keefe, Ed (18 August 2017a). Members of White House Presidential Arts Commission Resigning to Protest Trump's Comments.' *The Washington Post*. Retrieved https://www.washingtonpost.com/news/powerpost/wp/2017/08/18/members-of-white-house-presidential-arts-commission-resign-to-protest-trumps-comments/. Accessed 20 April 2020.

O'Keefe, Ed (18 August 2017b). Members of the President's Commission on Arts & Humanities Resignation Letter to President Trump. *Scribd*. Retrieved from https://www.scribd.com/document/356620864/Members-of-the-President-s-Commission-on-Arts-Humanities-resignation-letter-to-President-Trump. Accessed 20 April 2020.

O'Neill, S. A. & Schmidt, P. (2017). Arts Education in Canada and the United States. In G. Barton & M. Baguley (Eds.). *The Palgrave Handbook of Global Arts Education*. London: Palgrave Macmillan, 187–202.

Osborne, H. (1970). *The Art of Appreciation*. New York: Oxford University Press.

Peters, R. S. (1966). *Ethics and Education*. London: George Allen & Unwin.

Peters, R. S. (1973). The Justification of Education. In R. S. Peters (Ed.). *The Philosophy of Education*. Oxford: Oxford University Press, 239–67.

Phillips, S. (20 March 2019). Art under Threat: The Growing Crisis in Higher Education. *Royal Academy Magazine*. Retrieved from https://www.royalacademy.org.uk/article/art-under-threat-crisis-britain-higher-education. Accessed 7 May 2020.

Posner, R. (1997). Against Ethical Criticism. *Philosophy and Literature*, 21(1): 1–27.

Posner, R. (1998). Against Ethical Criticism: Part Two. *Philosophy and Literature*, 22(2): 394–412.

President's Committee on the Arts and the Humanities (PCAH) (May 2011). *Reinvesting in Arts Education: Winning America's Future through Creative Schools*. Washington, DC. Available via www.pcah.gov.

Pring, R. A. (1976). *Knowledge and Schooling*. London: Open Books.

Read, H. (1958). *Education through Art*. New York: Pantheon Books.

Read, H. (1964). *Art and Education*. Melbourne: Cheshire.

Redfern, H. B. (1986). *Questions in Aesthetic Education*. Boston: Allen Unwin.

Reiss, M. J. & White, J. (2013). *An Aims-based Curriculum: The Significance of Human Flourishing for Schools*. London: IOE Press.

Riefenstahl, L. (1935) Dir. *Triumph of the Will*. Film.

Robeyns, I. & Byskov, M. F. (2023). The Capability Approach. In E. N. Zalta (Ed.). *The Stanford Encyclopedia of Philosophy*. Retrieved from https://plato.stanford.edu/archives/sum2023/entries/capability-approach/. Accessed 17 August 2023.

Rosen, M. (1 September 2019). Term Is Starting – And English Schools Must Tackle Their Arts Emergency. *The Guardian*. Retrieved from https://www.theguardian.com/commentisfree/2019/sep/01/term-starting-english-schools-arts-emergency-subjects

Ross, N. (2017). *The Philosophy and Politics of Aesthetic Experience*. Cham, Switzerland: Palgrave Macmillan.

Saito, Y. (2007). *Everyday Aesthetics*. Oxford: Oxford University Press.

Saito, Y. (2015). Aesthetics of the Everyday. In E. N. Zalta (Ed.). *The Stanford Encyclopedia of Philosophy*. Retrieved from https://plato.stanford.edu/archives/win2015/entries/aesthetics-of-everyday/. Accessed 22 November 2019.

Schiller, F. (1795/1954). *Letters on the Aesthetic Education of Man*. E. M. Wilkinson and L. A. Willoughby (Trans.). Oxford: Oxford University Press. https://global.oup.com/academic/product/on-the-aesthetic-education-of-man-9780198157861?cc=gb&lang=en&.

Schindler, I., Hosoya, G., Menninghaus, W., Beermann, U., Wagner, V., Eid, M., & Scherer, K. R. (2017). Measuring Aesthetic Emotions: A Review of the Literature and a New Assessment Tool. *PLoS ONE*, 12(6): 1–45: e0178899.

Schinkel, A. (2017). The Educational Importance of Deep Wonder. *Journal of Philosophy of Education*, 51(2): 538–53.

Schinkel, A. (2018). Wonder and Moral Education. *Educational Theory*, 68(1): 31–48.

Schinkel, A. (2019). Presentation Wonderful Education Project. *Wonder, Education, and Human Flourishing* Conference, Hotel CASA, Amsterdam, 5–6 April 2019.

School Curriculum and Standards Authority (SCSA) (2019). 2019 Visual Arts ATAR course examination 2019 Marking Key. *Government of Western Australia*. Retrieved from https://senior-secondary.scsa.wa.edu.au/further-resources/past-atar-course-exams/visual-arts-past-atar-course-exams. Accessed 7 May 2020.

Sharp, C. & Métais, J. (2000). *The Arts, Creativity and Cultural Education: An International Perspective*. London: Qualifications and Curriculum Authority.

Shelley, J. (2017). The Concept of the Aesthetic. *The Stanford Encyclopedia of Philosophy* (Winter 2017 Edition), E. N. Zalta (Ed.). Retrieved from https://plato.stanford.edu/archives/win2017/entries/aesthetic-concept/

Sibley, F. (1956). Aesthetic and Non-aesthetic. *Philosophical Review*, 74: 135–59.

Sibley, F. (1965). Aesthetic and Non-aesthetic. *The Philosophical Review*, 74(2) (April): 135–59. https://doi.org/10.2307/2183262.

Snow, N. (2015). Generativity and Flourishing. *Journal of Moral Education*, 44(3): 263–77.

Sontag, S. (2007). An Argument about Beauty. In P. Dilonardo & A. Jump (Eds.). *At the Same Time: Essays and Speeches*. New York: Farrar Straus Giroux, 3–13.

Stewart, M. G. (2005). *Rethinking Curriculum in Art*. Maine: Davis Publications.

Stolnitz, J. (1960). *Aesthetics and Philosophy of Art Criticism*. Boston, MA: Houghton Mifflin, 32–42.

Tambling, P. & Bacon, S. (30 March 2023). *The Arts in Schools: Foundations for the Future*. A New Direction, Calouste Gulbenkian Foundation. Retrieved from https://www.anewdirection.org.uk/the-arts-in-schools. Accessed 20 August 2023.

Taylor, P. (Ed.) (1996). *Researching Drama and Arts Education*. London: The Falmer Press.

TES. Times Educational Supplement Magazine (22 August 2022). GCSEs 2022: EBacc Is 'Done for' as MLF Take-up Stalls, Says Exam Expert by Matilda Martin. Retrieved from https://www.tes.com/magazine/news/secondary/gcses-2022-ebacc-done-mfl-take-stalls-says-exams-expert

The Maxine Greene High School for Imaginative Inquiry (2022). New York, USA. Retrieved from https://www.mghs.nyc/apps/pages/index.jsp?uREC_ID=1058077&type=d&pREC_ID=1354823

The Maxine Greene Institute (2022). New York, USA. Retrieved from https://maxinegreene.org/about/maxine-greene/biography

The Policy Circle (2022). The Creative Economy. Retrieved from https://www.thepolicycircle.org/minibrief/the-creative-economy/. Accessed 18 February 2023.

Twain, M. (1884). *Adventures of Huckleberry Finn*. London: Chatto & Windus/orig. Charles L. Webster and Company.

UK Government (March 2016). *The Culture White Paper*. Department for Culture, Media and Sport.

UK Government (May 2019). *Changing Lives: The Social Impact of Participation in Culture and Sport*. Department for Culture, Media and Sport. Retrieved from https://publications.parliament.uk/pa/cm201719/cmselect/cmcumeds/734/73402.htm

Weber, B. (4 June 2014). Maxine Greene, 96, Dies; Education Theorist Saw Arts as Essential. Maxine Greene Obituary. *New York Times*. Retrieved from https://www.nytimes.com/2014/06/05/nyregion/maxine-greene-teacher-and-educational-theorist-dies-at-96.html

WeCreate (2018). Creative Industries Add $3.5 billion to NZ's GDP & WeCreate.org.nz Formed to Champion the Creative Sector. Retrieved from https://wecreate.org.nz/427/. Accessed 18 February 2023.

WeCreate (2022). Submission to *Increasing Value from Government Investment in the NZ Screen Production Grant*. Written by Victoria Blood, Auckland, New Zealand. Retrieved from https://wecreate.org.nz/wp-content/uploads/2023/02/WeCreate-SPG-Review-Submission-Dec-2022.pdf. Accessed 20 February 2023.

Weitz, M. (1956). The Role of Theory in Aesthetics. *The Journal of Aesthetics and Art Criticism*, 15(1): 27–35.

Weitz, M. (2004). The Role of Theory in Aesthetics. In P. Lamarque & S. H. Olsen (Eds.). *Aesthetics and the Philosophy of Art: The Analytic Tradition*. Oxford: Blackwell, 12–18.

White, J. (1973). *Towards a Compulsory Curriculum*. London: Routledge & Kegan Paul.

White, J. (2011). *Exploring Well-being in Schools: A Guide to Making Children's Lives More Fulfilling*. London: Routledge.

Wilde, O. (1891). *The Picture of Dorian Gray*. New York: W. W. Norton & Company, Inc.

Wilson, J. (1979). *Preface to the Philosophy of Education*. London: Routledge & Kegan Paul.

Wimsatt, W. K. & Beardsley, M. C. (1946). The Intentional Fallacy. *The Sewanee Review*, 54(3): 468–88.

Winner, E., Goldstein, T., & Vincent-Lancrin, S. (2013). *Art for Art's Sake? The Impact of Arts Education, Educational Research and Innovation*. Paris: OECD Publishing. Retrieved from http://dx.doi.org/10.1787/9789264180789-en

Wolcott, A. (1990). Aesthetic Experience: Is It Viable in Contemporary Education? *Marilyn Zurmuehlin Working Papers in Art Education*, 8: 97–103.

Wolcott, A. (1996). Is What You See What You Get? A Postmodern Approach to Understanding Works of Art. *Studies in Art Education*, 37(2): 69–79.

Wollstonecraft, M. (1792/2004). *A Vindication of the Rights of Woman: With Strictures on Political and Moral Subjects*. London: Penguin Books.

York, A. (3 November 1997). The Fourth 'R' in Education: Reading, Writing, Arithmetic and Art. Address Delivered to the Center for Constructive Alternatives, Art and Moral Imagination, Hillsdale College, Michigan. Reprinted in *Vital Speeches of the Day* (1998), 64(9): 274–9.

Young, J. O. (2005). *Aesthetics: Critical Concepts in Philosophy*. London: Routledge.

Index

aesthetic(s) 1, 36–7, 61, 70, 89, 131
   common-denominator 133
   and ethics 111, 128, 132, 140, 143
   experiences 1, 3–4, 7, 36–9, 50, 69–70, 81–5, 91–2, 99, 103, 105–7, 112–13, 125, 133, 138, 145, 149–50, 151 n.1
   literacy 84, 98
   and moral education 141–4
   responses 79, 96
   value 1, 7, 15, 38, 102, 122, 124, 128, 131–3, 135–8, 144, 149
aesthetica 36
   and *eudaimonia* 85–92
aesthetic education 2, 36, 67–8, 72, 74–6, 92, 101, 103, 106–7, 150
   benefit of 99
   cognitive outcomes 73, 127
   instrumental defences 5
aestheticism 5–6, 131–3, 136, 138, 140, 144
   educational implications of 134–5, 144
   and ethicism 132
Albanese, A. 31
American Academy of Arts & Sciences 18, 151 n.2
Anatolitis, E. 31
Anderson, M. 22–3
Annual Arts in Schools Reports (New York City) 18–19
anti-instrumentalization 117–20
Aotearoa New Zealand, creative industries 126
Aristotle 46–7, 78
art(s) 3, 18, 36, 39, 41, 51, 61, 74, 76, 83, 121–3, 129, 141, 148, 150
   and beauty 36–7
   class 100, 143, 150
   connections and relationships 15–16
   and design programme 12
   and education 10 (*see also* arts education)
   expressivist view of 39–45

instinct 77–81
intrinsic value of 148–9
literacy 41–3
and literature 46
making and cognition 59, 65
media 36, 38–43, 45, 51, 81, 98, 114, 144
as moral formation 45–51, 77, 127
objects 70, 72, 77, 79–80, 83–5, 96, 101, 105–6, 148, 151 n.1
and perception 83
qua work of 100, 132, 137–8
Art for Art's Sake?: The Impact of Arts Education (OECD) 123
artistic depiction 85
artistic literacy 58, 60–1, 73
artistic perception 15
artists 13, 16, 39, 43, 81, 98, 117, 122, 134, 136, 142, 148
   and community 30
   creative nature of 6, 85, 131, 144
arts-based research 4, 54, 64–5
Arts Council England 30
arts education 1–2, 10, 12, 20, 32, 35, 41, 54, 65, 75, 111, 119, 123, 127, 129, 138, 144
   instrumental justification 106, 109, 113, 120, 122
   intrinsic value 1, 5
   policy and practice (*see* policies/practices (arts education))
   research on 123
   and specific skills 123
Arts Education in Public Elementary and Secondary Schools: 1999–2000 report 18
The Arts in Schools: Foundations for the Future 28–9
Arts Policy Council 20
artworks 36, 44, 50–1, 55, 76, 80, 82, 90–1, 97, 106, 111–12, 114, 128, 143, 148, 152 n.4

and aesthetic experience 37
artists and 6, 134, 142, 148
determination and patience 98–9
education of artists and audiences 39
ethical evaluation of 135
intrinsic value of 105–6, 114, 141
moral judgements/value of 142, 144
narrative 3, 45, 48–50, 96, 101, 135–6, 139–41
object 39
sensual and erotic 112
utterances and experiences 41
value and connection 5, 77, 104, 111, 113, 131, 133–4, 142–4
worthwhile activity 98–101, 105, 112, 114, 150
Auden, W. H. 131
Australia 30, 35, 55
   creative economy 125–6
   The Curriculum: The Arts 23
   industry's economic contribution 31
   national arts curriculum 11–12, 85
   policies/practices (arts education) 2, 9, 21–4, 54–5
Australia Council for Educational Research (ACER) 23
autonomism. *See* aestheticism

Bamford, A. 9–10, 18, 29
Barone, T., *Arts Based Research* 64
Baumgarten, A. G. 36
Beardsley, M. 37–8, 54, 82
Bell, C. 38–40, 133
Biesta, G. 44, 119, 122
   ambition of education 121
   instrumental justifications 119–20
Boethius, *The Consolation of Philosophy* 119
Booth, W. C. 131, 135
Brighouse, H. 101–2, 107, 152 n.2
   educational goods and capacities 101
Broudy, H. S. 42–3, 151 n.3
Byskov, M. F. 89

California, arts education in 15–16
Carr, D. 46–7
Carroll, N. 131, 136, 143, 153 n.1
Changing Lives: the social impact of participation in culture and sport report 24–6

Chapman, S. 22
cognition/cognitivism 55, 57–61, 69, 74, 83, 91
Collingwood, R. G. 39–40, 151 n.2
Collinson, D. 36–7
   aesthetic contemplation 83
The Commission on the Arts 18, 151 n.2
communication 42, 49, 51, 60, 115
compulsory aesthetic education 3–4, 36, 51, 53–4, 76, 91, 93, 104, 106–7, 109, 124
compulsory arts education 3, 18, 24, 33, 35, 45, 105, 107
Conway, C. M. 23
cost-benefit analyses 32
creative arts 28–9, 58, 125, 127
creative expression/self-expression 3, 11, 15–16, 35, 40, 43, 45, 112, 122, 127, 134, 143–4, 147
creative industries, economic value of 30, 125–8
Creative Industries Federation 30
creative skills 126
Culture White Paper (2016) 25
Cunningham, S. 126

defences of aesthetic education 3–4, 32, 36, 52, 54, 75–6, 91, 95, 105–7, 109, 111, 128
   Eisner 56–66, 72
   Greene 66–72
   instrumental (*see* instrumental defences of education)
defences of arts education 3, 32–3, 35, 40, 51–3, 76, 107, 128
   Eisner 56–66
   Greene 66–72
Devereaux, M. 131, 136, 140
Dewey, J. 4, 38, 54, 67–70, 152 n.5
   Art as Experience 81–2
   everyday aesthetics 152 n.5
Dickie, G. 38, 152 n.3
discipline-based art education (DBAE) 4, 17, 32, 54–5, 65, 72–3
   disciplines 56
   and language 56
Don Giovanni (Mozart) 80, 84
Duncan, A. 20
Dutton, D. 4
   The Art Instinct 78

Eaton, M. M. 79, 83
educational curricula 2–3, 10, 14, 16, 56, 73, 85, 123, 127
educators. *See* teachers, arts
Egan, K. 57
Eisner, E. 3–4, 52, 54, 56–61, 72–4, 75, 105, 127
   academic disciplines 65–6
   The Arts and the Creation of Mind 62–3
   Arts Based Research 64
   cognition 58–60
   expressive outcomes 57
   instructional objectives 57
   knowledge 57–9
   null curriculum 61
   problem-solving objectives 57
   Ten Lessons the Arts Teach 62–4
   time 62
Elementary and Secondary Education Act (1965) 18
empiricism, aesthetic value 38
'Engage. Reflect. Act.' 142
English Baccalaureate (EBacc) 26–9
environmental education 99–100, 121
ethical attention 3
ethicism 6, 132, 136–7, 141, 144
   moral flaws as aesthetic flaws 137–40
   value of artwork 131
eudaimonia (flourishing) life 32, 45, 54, 66, 74, 76–7, 85–92, 95–6, 98–102, 104–9, 112–14, 127–8, 148–50, 152 n.8
Evaluation of School-based Arts Education Programmes in Australian Schools 23
Every Student Succeeds Act 18
Ewing, R. 23, 30
existential experience 44–5
expressive outcomes 57
expressivist view of art 39–45, 122

Feminist Art Coalition (FAC) 142
Fletcher, P. 31
flourishing life. *See eudaimonia* (flourishing) life
Frankena, W. K. 105
Friend, D. 143
Fry, R. 39–40

Gaut, B. 136
Gibson, R. 22–3
good quality arts education 2, 10, 17, 35

Greene, M. 3–4, 38, 43–4, 52, 54, 56, 66–75, 84, 97, 105
   aesthetic experiences 69–70
   'The artistic-aesthetic and curriculum' 73
   art objects 70, 72
   importance of teaching 72
   sensory experiences 71
   Variations on a Blue Guitar: The Lincoln Center Institute Lectures on Aesthetic Education 67–8
Guerrilla Girls 141

Hand, M. 152 n.7
high art 39–40, 92, 133, 151 n.2
Hill, L. 26
Hirst, P. H. 152 n.7
historical and cultural context 3, 15–16, 35, 55, 77
human flourishing 149. *See also eudaimonia* (flourishing) life

instructional objective 57
instrumental defences of education 5
   extrinsic benefits 120–4
   against instrumentalization 117–20, 122
   intrinsic and extrinsic benefits 124–7
   non-instrumental attitude (Peters) 114–17
   worthwhile activities 114
internalist theory 38
International Baccalaureate 9
internationalization 10
interpretation of arts 41–2

Jackson, F. 90
James, H. 47, 49
J. Paul Getty Trust Foundation 17, 54
Judson, G. 57

Kant, I. 117
   formula of humanity 117
   utilitarianism 118
Kearns, L.-L. 128
Kemp, G. 152 n.3
Klein, N. 118
Knott, J. 27
knowledge 11–12, 36, 55, 57–61, 65, 84, 108
   as justified true belief (JTB) 60
   theoretical 56, 116
Kristjánsson, K. 89–90, 149–50

literature 46, 104–6, 134, 136, 139–40, 152 n.7
Lorde, A. 147

MacDonald, D. 151 n.2
MacIntyre, A. 47
mass art 44, 96, 145, 152 n.2
Maxine Greene High School for Imaginative Inquiry 67
Mill, J. S. 103
moderate autonomism 131, 133, 138
moderate moralism 131, 136–7, 140–1, 153 n.1
moral education/formation, art as 45–51, 77, 91, 107, 127, 133
    aesthetic and 141–4
    etiquette and 47
    narrative art in 105
    phronesis 47
    real life moral dilemmas 46–7
    schools 50
    stories and images 49
    virtues 46
Morrison, S. 30–1
Mrdak, M. 31
Murdoch, I. 47–9, 139–40
music curriculum, UK 13–14

Nabokov, V., *Lolita* 132
national arts curriculum 56, 77
    Australia 11–12
    UK 12–14
National Assessment Program – Literacy and Numeracy (*NAPLAN*) 22
national testing on literacy/numeracy 17
naturalistic objection 4, 95–101, 108
Nazism 140, 143
New York City
    Annual Arts in Schools Reports 18–19
    New York State Education Law 18
No Child Left Behind Act (*2001 & 2002*) 18
Noddings, N. 59
null curriculum 61
Nussbaum, M. 4, 47–9, 85–6, 105, 131, 139–40, 147
    human capabilities 86–9, 91
    Senses, Imagination, and Thought 4, 87

Obama, B. 20
objections to aesthetic education 4, 108
    naturalistic 4–5, 95–101, 108
    subjectivity 5, 95, 101–8
O'Neill, S. A. 21
Orwell, G. 131
    1984 140

Peters, R. S. 99, 122
    Ethics and Education 114
    'The Justification of Education' 115
    non-instrumental attitude 114–17
Phillips, S. 28
policies/practices (arts education) 2, 11–17, 53–4, 72
    in Australia 2, 9, 17, 21–4, 54–5
    gap between 23, 29, 35
    historical influences on 54–6
    in the UK 2, 9, 17, 24–9, 54–5
    in the United States of America 2, 9, 17, 18–21, 54–5
Posner, R. 131, 134–6
potential space of aesthetic activity 48
President's Committee on the Arts and Humanities (PCAH) 19–21
Pring, R. A. 152 n.7
problem-solving objectives 57

quality, arts education 2, 10, 17, 29, 35, 134

radical autonomism 132–3
Radio National, *Books and Arts* 153 n.3
Reiss, M. J. 102, 104–7, 152 nn.1–2
Riefenstahl, L., *Triumph of the Will* 137, 140, 143
Robeyns, I. 89
Rosen, M. 27
Ross, N. 125

Saatchi gallery, London 141
Schmidt, P. 21
school-aged students 3–4, 7, 19, 33, 93, 102, 107, 124, 150
    primary and secondary 9, 13, 17
    skills and techniques 102
schools 148
    funding 19
    local artists and and businesspeople 16
    moral formation 50

science, technology, engineering and mathematics (STEM) subjects 1, 11, 17, 77, 128
self-expression 39–41, 44–5, 51, 53, 75, 91, 107
   as catharsis 43
   creative 3, 11, 15–16, 35, 40, 43, 45, 112, 122, 127
   and moral formation 77, 127
Sibley, F. 37
skills and techniques, artistic 2, 36, 42, 44, 54–5, 78, 81, 98–9, 101–2, 148, 150
skill set 84, 112
socio-politico-economic-ethical context 44, 51, 147
Sontag, S. 48, 91
statutory aesthetic education 69, 108
student flourishing 149–50
subjectivity objection 5, 95, 101–8

Tate Modern, London 141
   'Women and Power' 142
Taylor, P., *Researching Drama and Arts Education* 73
teachers, arts 5–6, 11, 18–19, 23, 25, 27–30, 71, 84, 89, 99–100, 103, 107, 128, 132, 144–5
Times Educational Supplement (TES) Magazine 27
Trump, D. 21
Twain, M., *Huckleberry Finn* 132

UK (England)
   Creative Industries 126
   disadvantaged students 17, 151 n.1
   Education Act (2002) 85
   music curriculum 13–14
   national curriculum 12–13
   policies/practices (arts education) 9, 24–9, 35, 54–5
   registrations for arts GCSEs 26
   teachers of arts subjects 27–8
The United States of America
   creative arts 125
   networking language 16
   New York State Education Law 18
   policies/practices (arts education) 18–21, 54–5
   public education 14
   'Unite the Right rally' 21
   U.S. Bureau of Economic Analysis 125
   visual and performing arts (California) 15–16
values of arts 1–2, 5, 7, 9, 22, 25–6, 31, 70, 111, 117, 124–5, 127, 133, 136, 144, 148, 150
visual and performing arts curriculum, California 14–16

Wagner, R. 143
Weitz, M. 36, 68–9
White, J. 98–9, 102, 104–7, 152 nn.1–2
Wilde, O. 131
   The Picture of Dorian Gray 135
Wilson, J. 152 n.7
Wittgenstein, L., family resemblances 36
Wolcott, A. 55
Wollstonecraft, M. 45

www.ingramcontent.com/pod-product-compliance
Lightning Source LLC
Chambersburg PA
CBHW052126300426
44116CB00010B/1794